Praise for Sarah Harrison Smith's
The Fact Checker's Bible

"A how-to manual on not making mistakes. . . . An accuracy Bible."
—*The Boston Globe*

"Expert advice, long overdue. Fact checkers, the battlefield angels of print, save civilization from Babeldom every day. Sarah Harrison Smith should feel chuffed (see inside)." —Richard Rhodes

"How are readers to know whether the reviews, news accounts and feature stories they read are accurate, both factually and contextually? Asked more philosophically, how do readers know they are learning the Truth? The truth is, they do not, and cannot, know completely. But, when reading some magazines and some books, readers who care about accuracy and Truth are served by an unseen ally. Within the journalism world, that ally is called a fact checker. . . . Wise. . . . Smith knows a lot about working with freelance authors, staff writers and editors." —*San Francisco Chronicle*

"Full of useful advice. . . . Smith takes an inside look at libel laws, plagiarism and . . . fabrication. She discusses in particular how to judge the accuracy of various sources and where to find reliable facts. And she enlivens her account with anecdotes, from Stephen Glass to Edna St. Vincent Millay." —*The Wall Street Journal*

Sarah Harrison Smith

The Fact Checker's Bible

Sarah Harrison Smith has been a fact checker at *The New Yorker* and head of checking at *The New York Times Magazine,* where she is now editorial manager. She lives in New York City.

hostile
witness

The
Fact
Checker's
Bible

A GUIDE TO GETTING IT RIGHT

SARAH HARRISON SMITH

ANCHOR BOOKS
A Division of Random House, Inc.
New York

Grateful acknowledgment is made to Farrar, Straus and Giroux,
LLC, for permission to reprint the following: Excerpt from
"The Los Angeles Notebook" from *Slouching Towards Bethle-
hem* by Joan Didion. Copyright © 1966, 1968, renewed 1996
by Joan Didion. Excerpt from "The Woods from Hog Wallow"
from *The Pine Barrens* by John McPhee. Copyright © 1967,
1968 by John McPhee. Reprinted by permission of Farrar,
Straus and Giroux, LLC.

Library of Congress Cataloging-in-Publication Data
Smith, Sarah Harrison.
The fact checker's bible : a guide to getting it right /
Sarah Harrison Smith.—1st Anchor Books ed.
p.   cm.
Includes bibliographical references.
ISBN 0-385-72106-4
1. Editing.   I. Title.
PN162.S58 2004
808'.027—dc22   2003063896

www.anchorbooks.com

Printed in the United States of America
10   9   8   7   6   5   4   3   2

For Martin Baron and Peter Canby
with admiration and gratitude

Contents

Introduction   3

    Why Is Fact-Checking Necessary?

    Establishing Institutional Standards

1. Is That a Fact?   16

    How to Read a Piece for the First Time

    What to Notice During a First Reading

    The Second Reading

    Determining What to Check in Nonfiction

    When the Author Is an Expert

    Checking Reviews

2. Source Material   25

    The Author's Responsibility to the Checker

    Assessing Source Materials

    Newspapers

    LexisNexis, Factiva, and Other

        Online News Databases

    The Web

    Books

    Human Sources

3. Due Decorum: Working with Authors and Editors   41
    The Delicate Balance
    How to Get Your Relationship with the Author
        Off to a Good Start and How to Spot
        Checking Problems Early
    Time Management
    What to Check First
    Delegating Work to Other Checkers
    Presenting Your Queries and Corrections to the Author
    When You and the Author Don't Agree
    Leaving Facts "On Author"
    When Fact-Checking Becomes Research
    Working Amicably with the Editor
    When You and the Editor Don't Agree

4. Checking Quotations and Talking to Sources   64
    Checking Facts Within Quotes
    Relying on the Author's Notes to Check Quotations
    Relying on Tapes and Transcripts
    Checking with Sources by Telephone
    Checking with the Source by Letter, Fax, or E-mail
    On the Record, Off the Record, On Background,
        and Not for Attribution
    Anonymous Sources and Disguised Identities
    Dialect, Grammar, and Accents
    Checking Diaries for Publication
    Permissions and Fair Use of Quotations
    Quoting Letters

5. Plagiarism and Fabrication   87

Defining Plagiarism

Plagiarism and Computers

The Too-Good Memory

Self-Plagiarism

How Fact Checkers Can Catch Plagiarism
    Before It Is Published

Use of the Internet and Nexis

Checking for Plagiarism of Ideas

Intentional Plagiarism

Fabrication

The Legacy of the New Journalism

Fabrication's Warning Signs

"Innocent" Fabricators

6. Libel   103

Defining Libel

Who Can Sue

What Is Defamatory

Actual Malice

The Fact-Checking Process as a Safeguard
    Against Liability

The Problem with Memorandums

Foreign Libel Law

7. Checking Fiction and Poetry   120

Real People and Fictional Characters

When Real Names Appear in Fiction and Poetry

The Potential for Libel

When an Author Borrows Characters from
    Another Author's Work

Fiction and Poetry Set in a Specific Historical Period
Locations: Real Places and Fictional Places
Flora and Fauna
Objects

8. Special Fact-Checking   131

Checking Drawings, Cartoons, and Paintings
Checking Photography
The Importance of Looking at Art Carefully
Dates of Photographs
Analyzing the Implications of Photographs and Art
Checking Captions and Headlines
Checking Maps
Checking Video Documentaries
Fact-Checking a News Program
Getting Legal Documents from Courts
Fact-Checking Songs and Lyrics
Checking Letters to the Editor

9. Checking Resources   149

Assessing the Credibility of Research Materials
Assessing the Reliability of Reference Books
Assessing the Research Value of Internet Sites
Creating a Checking Rolodex or Source List
How Specific Publications and Resources Are Fact-Checked
    The New York Times
    The Washington Post
    Time
    The Economist
    Scientific American
    World Almanac

Recommended Sources

    Advertising

    Art and Architecture

    Ballet

    Business

    Food

    General Reference

    History

    Libraries

    Literature

    Medicine

    Military Information

    Movies and Movie Actors

    Music

        Rock 'n' Roll

        Songs and Lyrics

        Music Licensing Companies

    People

    Photography

    Quotations

    Radio

    Sports

    Television

    Theater

    U.S. Government

    Wine

    The World

Bibliography   171

Acknowledgments

I owe great thanks to my former colleagues at *The New Yorker* checking department and my new coworkers at *The New York Times Magazine*, from whom I have learned so much.

I must also thank the journalists who have reported on fact-checking in the news, particularly those at the *Columbia Journalism Review, Brill's Content,* and *The New York Times.*

John Thornton of the Spieler Agency came up with the idea for *The Fact Checker's Bible* and was extremely helpful throughout the proposal and writing of the book. Alice van Straalen, my editor at Anchor Books, was enormously patient, encouraging, and thoughtful. I am very grateful to them both.

My mother, Marlis Smith, who as a young woman worked at the information bureau of the New York *Daily News,* helped to care for my infant daughter so that I could have more time to write. My husband, David Yezzi, was supportive in innumerable ways and, as a former head of fact-checking at *The New York Observer,* was an ideal person to talk to about the issues.

Many people generously discussed their experiences in fact-checking, writing, editing, or the practice of media law. In particular, I would like to thank Linda Amster, Michael Anderson, Greta Austin, Martin Baron, Sandra Baron, Jeffrey Blum, Lois Smith Brady, Patricia Brown, Peter Canby, Chris Carduff, Deirdre Casper, Devereux Chatillon, Susan Choi, Russ Clarkson, Anne Colby, John Cotter, Cynthia Cotts, Amy Davidson, Byron Dobell, Elizabeth Dobell, John Dorfman, Jillian Dunham, Liz Duvall, Emily Eakin, Blake Eskin, Marion Farrier, David Ferguson, Mike Fleming, Nancy Franklin, Jeff Franks, George Freeman, Paul Gallagher, Kevin Goering, Kim Grad, Dade Hayes, Virginia Heffernan, Carol Howard, Dorothy Ingebretson, Esther Kartiganer, Dan Kaufman, Johanna Keller, David Kirkpatrick, David Korzenik, Hilton Kramer, Thomas Kunkel, Mary LaMotte, Michael LaRaque, Bruce Lazarus, William Lin, Sara Lippincott, William Littler, Clark Lombardi, Robert Mackey, Kee Malesky, Charles Martin, David McCraw, Bill McGeveran, Renée Michael, Annette Miller, Anne Mortimer-Maddox, Eric Nash, Jim Oberman, Cynthia Ozick, Robert Read, Mandy Reilly, Lee Riffaterre, Nandi Rodrigo, Dana Rodriguez, Lesley Rogers, Megan Rosenfield, Betty Satterwhite, Robert Scheffler, Liesl Schillinger, Dan Schlenoff, Ellen Scordato, Allan Siegal, Spencer Smith, Jim Steinblatt, Anne Stringfield, Julie Tate, Jeff Toobin, Calvin Trillin, Ken Tucker, Nola Tully, Robert Walsh, Greg Welch, Av Westin, Eileen Whitfield, Margot Williams, Jane Wulf, Jonathan Zittrain, and the staff of the New York Society Library.

The Fact Checker's Bible

Introduction

Why Is Fact-Checking Necessary?

Depending upon your areas of knowledge, you'll be bothered by different sorts of errors in print. You are likely to notice mistakes in a short story set in your hometown, in a profile of a business or a person you know well, in a review of a book you've read—or worse, written—or in a feature about a place or subject you've studied. Some errors are benign and positively enjoyable to anyone they don't malign, and spotting errors can become something of a sport. As Cullen Murphy noted in *The Atlantic Monthly*, the section newspapers allot to corrections is one of the most entertaining to read. "What most readers take away from such columns is not appreciation for the retrospective accuracy but gratitude for the original mistake." (For people who really enjoy a good error, I recommend *Kill Duck Before Serving*, Linda Amster and Dylan Loeb McClain's funny collection of *New York Times* corrections. The *Times* established a section for corrections in 1972 and since then has been delighting and horrifying readers with periodic handfuls of howlers.) I admit to feeling a little schadenfreude when I see misidentifications of people and places in photographs. It doesn't seem to matter much most of the time, particularly when the error is obvious. It merely embarrasses the publication and its editors (the latter, for the most part, anonymous to most readers in any case).

Some errors detract more seriously from the reputation of the writer, or at least, his or her credibility in the reader's eyes. The jacket copy for Joseph Epstein's book *Narcissus Leaves the Pool* compares him to Hazlitt, Mencken, and Montaigne. But on page 145 of this collection of essays, Epstein defines *chuffed*, a word he says is new to him, as meaning "irritated, disgruntled, more than a little displeased." He's wrong. Merriam-Webster defines *chuffed* as "proud, satisfied." It's a small error. To those readers who notice it, however, it undermines faith in Epstein's erudition. If this one word is defined as opposite to its actual meaning, what else in the essays could be wrong? To my mind, Epstein should have been protected from this embarrassment by his publishers. An editor or fact checker should have taken a moment to check *chuffed.*

Some writers are intentionally ambiguous about the line between fiction and fact. There's a virtue to allowing authors to filter reality through their imaginations, and that tempering ought to be respected and permitted. I would argue that blending fiction and fact is fine so long as everyone involved in the production of the work knows which is which and the reader is made aware that he's not reading straight fact. Fact-checking can help to delineate the boundaries between fact and fiction and, of course, ensure that the facts intended to correspond to objective fact are accurate.

The issues are different, however, when the writing in question is reportage. Documenting real events is serious. The most interesting pieces are often the most difficult to confirm, and when checkers are unable to speak directly to sources, much of the burden of verification falls on the author. This always involves some risk. Michael Finkel got away with creating a composite character as the protagonist for his *New York Times Magazine* story "Is Youssouf Malé a Slave?", blending the experiences of a number of young men in similar situations into a portrait of one. The photograph the author provided to accompany the piece was identified as being of Youssouf Malé but was, in fact, of a boy named Madou Traoré. Other important facts in the story were shown to be incorrect after publication. Finkel's conflations and inventions were embarrassing to the *Times*, particularly because the magazine did attempt to fact check the story. If Finkel's reporting had been more reliable, the checking process might not have mattered so much. Finkel had published eight other pieces at the *Times* without any checking problems. In this case, however, the combination of a newspaper-style policy of not requiring authors to submit their notes and some seemingly insurmountable difficulties in communicating with sources in Mali led to an entire article—not just a few stray facts—slipping into publication without adequate corroboration.

The real trouble with errors, whether they are significant, as in Finkel's piece in the *Times Magazine*, or insubstantial, as in Epstein's essay, is that they cause readers to become cynical. As Sara Lippincott, a former head of fact-checking at *The New Yorker*, once said, "A little skepticism . . . is much to be desired, but if it is fed over and over again with a diet of misinformation, it eventually becomes cynicism, which is a different thing entirely. Then we are turned off. Then we cease to listen to each other at all, and so the journalist is in danger of becoming extinct—or ignored, which amounts to the same thing."

In the United States, the press receives some protection from damages when public figures or officials sue for libel. The protection, available only since the 1964 U.S. Supreme Court ruling in *New York Times v. Sullivan*, requires plaintiffs to prove that the defendant publication either was aware of the falsity of what it was about to print before going to press or at least had serious reason to doubt the validity of the facts. If prior knowledge or "reckless disregard" of falsehood can be proven, the defendant can be found guilty of "actual malice." The court believed that the actual malice standard was in keeping with the intentions of the framers of the Constitution, who protected the freedom of the press in the First Amendment.

Americans have more respect for journalists than do readers in other nations, and the court allows the media to make innocent mistakes and not be punished. But the latitude the press is granted is also a responsibility. If authors and publishers let too many errors slip through, the presumption of the good intentions and integrity of the author—particularly the investigative reporter—will begin to disintegrate, and the public will begin to wish that we had a libel law more like that of the United Kingdom, which presumes that a contested statement is false unless proven true by the defending author or editor. There, journalism is often regarded as an irresponsible profession for dilettantes, and cynicism runs high. Fact-checking can save publishers and writers from libel damages. More importantly, checking can save the press's reputation from becoming tainted by cynicism when readers become hardened to errors, both large and small.

I've been lucky enough to work at two of the best magazines published in English. I was a checker at *The New Yorker* for about five years, and since August 2002 I've headed the checking department at *The New York Times Magazine*. (I wrote the first drafts of this book between the two jobs.) Both magazines employ full-time fact checkers who check virtually every word that goes into print. The writers who publish in these magazines take their work very seriously, and they're very good at it. Nevertheless, without fact-checking, these two great magazines would have printed articles that referred to "islands off the coast of Switzerland" and described trips to "Helskinki." More significantly, their writers would have condemned men for crimes for which they had not yet stood trial, and a convicted killer would have been made a hero of sorts for the crime he claimed to have committed, the murder of his sister's rapist, who had knowingly infected her with HIV. This "hero" had actually been convicted of a different murder: burning a woman alive in an alley. Publications such as *The*

New Yorker and *The New York Times Magazine* use checkers because checkers make these kinds of "saves" all the time. The public's trust could not withstand more than an issue or two that had not been fact-checked. The errors would be too numerous, embarrassing, and legally dangerous.

It's easy to identify when fact-checking fails; that's what makes corrections so much fun to read. Fact-checking victories, on the other hand, are evanescent. They vanish from sight before the piece is published, and only the checker, author, and editor remember, for a week or two, that a different version of the story ever existed. I've noticed that fact checkers tend to want to hold on to the galleys and proofs on which they've made their corrections. In the end, these sheets of paper, covered with hastily written phone numbers, synopses of conversations, check marks, and corrections, are the only tangible evidence of the hard work that goes into protecting the reputations of good writers and publications.

Transitory victories notwithstanding, fact-checking is fascinating work. The people who are attracted to it were often good students who love to continue learning. They are quick studies who in one week can transform themselves from balletomanes to experts in the latest genetic research. Many fact checkers are also writers or writers-in-training. (The dean of the journalism school at the University of Maryland says he considers fact-checking such "excellent training" for writers that he uses advanced journalism students to check the school's magazine, *American Journalism Review*.) Other checkers are on the well-traveled road to becoming editors. Some do freelance fact-checking to pay their bills while they make films or do other creative projects on the side. Some are career checkers who have discovered that they excel at the odd amalgam of tasks that checking encompasses.

Fact-checking has a long history in American magazine publishing. The first fact checkers were probably those hired in the early 1920s by Briton Hadden and Henry Luce for their fledgling publication *Time*, which was founded in 1923. These checkers verified names, dates, and facts and marked news items for writers to use when compiling their stories. They were all female. (A number of early research departments, including that of *Reader's Digest*, were markedly discriminatory. Fact-checking was considered women's work.) A tongue-in-cheek memo written by *Time* editor Edward Kennedy, minus its patronizing tone, would be as applicable to checkers today as it was in its own time. He wrote:

> Checking is . . . sometimes regarded as a dull and tedious occupation, but such a conception of this position is extremely erroneous. Any bright girl who really applies herself to the handling of the checking problem can have a very pleasant time with it and fill the week with happy moments and memorable occasions. The most important point to remember in checking is that the writer is your natural enemy. He is trying to see how much he can get away with. Remem-

ber that when people write letters about mistakes, it is you who will be screeched at. So protect yourself. . . .

The New Yorker was launched a year after Time. Initially, the magazine was somewhat sloppy with the facts. As Ben Yagoda writes in his history of The New Yorker, its meticulous checking system didn't begin until 1927, when "a profile of Edna St. Vincent Millay was so riddled with errors that the poet's mother stormed into the magazine's offices and threatened to sue if an extensive correction was not run." (Poor Millay: At about the same time The New York Times maligned her with a gross typo, advertising her "immortal verse" as "immoral verse.") The New Yorker's founder, Harold Ross, had a passion for accuracy. His biographer Thomas Kunkel says that Ross's obsessive concern that the magazine be irrefutable was partly defensive. In its "Newsbreaks" section, The New Yorker ridiculed other publications' inaccuracies. Ross was afraid the magazine would be tarred with its own brush. In a 1927 memo he wrote: "What with our making fun of other publications and what with the nature of the magazine, 'The New Yorker' ought to be freer from typographical errors than any other publication. . . . A SPECIAL EFFORT SHOULD BE MADE TO AVOID MISTAKES IN 'THE NEW YORKER.'" By the mid-1970s, The New Yorker had seven checkers on staff. When Tina Brown became editor in 1992, there were eight. This number doubled during her tenure, partly as a result of an increase in the timely and controversial nature of the pieces published. In 2003, there were sixteen checkers at the magazine.

Time and *The New Yorker* began what would become a trend in American magazines. There are now fact-checking departments all over the country. While fear of lawsuits certainly motivates publishers to maintain these departments, most realize that they need checkers to keep their readers' good faith. Big errors may occasionally end up in court; small errors, such as wrong dates or incorrect name spellings, will be remarked on by thousands of people. If each reader begins to trust the publication a little less with every error, the eventual cost will be its reputation.

Fact checkers are everywhere, though many don't call themselves by that name. Editors, copy editors, writers, and researchers for print, radio, and even television verify facts as part of their jobs. Media that don't employ nominal fact checkers often divide the work of a fact checker among employees who do lots of other things, too. Radio and television tend not to be fact-checked in the manner described in this book. A number of reasons exist for the difference. Perhaps the most significant is that most broadcast programs do not have the kind of lead time that weekly and monthly print publications do. There simply isn't time for an extra step. But looking closely at reputable news programs, one can see that though there may not be any "fact checkers," a lot of fact-checking is being done, often by very senior staff. This is the case at *The NewsHour with Jim Lehrer*, discussed in Chapter Eight.

At a first-rate magazine, a checker will begin a checking

project by reading a piece carefully two or three times, underlining facts that need to be checked and thinking about any potential difficulties the piece presents. After conferring with the editor of the piece, he'll call or e-mail the author, asking for information about the sources the author used. He'll ask the author for notes, tapes, and any other material the author may have used in preparing the piece. The two will discuss a general plan for the checking. Then the checker will review the author's source material, read the notes, call the sources, find new ones, and generally do all he can to confirm the facts of the piece. When he has checked some portion of the piece, he and the editor may decide that it would be best for the changes to be put onto the version that the editor is working on. The checker will discuss his changes with the author and give his changes to the editor. The checker will continue to work until all the facts are checked, including any new facts that may be added by the author or editor during the period before the piece goes to press. The checker will also check any art, photographs, or additional text, such as captions and headlines, that will accompany the piece. On a complicated piece with legal ramifications he may work closely with the publication's legal counsel. Checking protocol varies, depending on each publication's institutional standards.

Establishing Institutional Standards

Although this book is for fact checkers and checking departments, good checking requires the cooperation of the entire office. Editors, copy editors, art editors, and production people all need to know what checking does and to understand the value of checking to each section of a publication. Authors and editors can be resistant to checking. It requires their attention and time to address checking concerns, when they are nearly always up to their necks doing their own work.

Fact-checking does put a burden on other members of the staff, but it is always worth it, because checking makes everyone involved in the editorial process look good. It helps ensure that the author doesn't make a fool of herself, that the art editor doesn't provide a picture of a yawl when the story concerns a ketch, and that the editor doesn't delete a passage that is crucial to the balance and fair reporting of the piece. If publishing were a leisurely venture and authors, art editors, copy editors, and features editors had months to finish work on a book, broadcast, or article, checkers might play a less dramatic role than they do now. But the market is competitive, and there's pressure to print or broadcast before a story is scooped elsewhere. In this atmosphere, checking is vital, because the quality of attention that other constituents of the publishing chain—the author, the copy editor, the editor—can give to the story is diminished by the exigencies of scheduling.

Establishing institutional standards for fact-checking requires the cooperation of the entire publication. It's not easy to improve standards and it takes time. In most cases, improvement is a matter of process and continuing communication among departments and within the checking department. For a checking department to function efficiently, checking procedures must be integrated into a publication's schedule so that checkers have enough time to check captions, headlines, and art as well as the article they accompany. There also has to be some provision for a crisis. If the checker can't contact a crucial source in time for the closing or discovers that the piece requires significant additional reporting, another piece should be available to run in place of the problematic one. Publications also need to be willing to pay for a sufficient number of checkers to do their work thoroughly within the time the schedule allows.

There are few, if any, absolute rules in fact-checking. Each piece requires a checker to take a slightly different approach. So many variables exist: the author, her reputation, her knowledge of the subject, the thoroughness of the reporting, the subject, the sensitivity of the subject, the quality of the source material provided by the author, the availability of other sources, and the time the schedule allows for checking. In checking departments, teaching tends to be a matter of gradual mentoring, occasional postmortem analyses of checking problems, and rare discussions of ethical and legal guidelines. It might take years for a checker to become fully competent to work on a broad range of challenging pieces.

It's an inefficient system, but department heads are caught in a bind. Checkers could assimilate more advice about checking methods if some recommendations were written down, but written protocols are a legal liability. Media lawyers have an aversion to seeing checking advice on paper. One says, "I don't like written guidelines. They can cause real problems because eventually they won't be followed." In a libel case, the plaintiff's lawyers will try to establish that the checker on the allegedly defamatory piece has departed from a standard method for checking. (This was an aspect of Jeffrey Masson's 1984–1994 libel case against *The New Yorker* magazine, Alfred A. Knopf, and Janet Malcolm.) *The Fact Checker's Bible* is a discussion of the issues that must be taken into account to do good fact-checking and recommends "best practices" for checkers in a form that is more expedient than word-of-mouth mentoring. Best practices represent a high standard that may not necessarily be the norm. Each piece requires different tactics; what should be constant from piece to piece is the checker's attention to all the facts and sensitivity to implication. The checker's eye must be naturally skeptical, but skepticism is not enough. It should also be informed.

1

Is That a Fact?

How to Read a Piece for the First Time

When you prepare to read any piece for fact-checking, make certain you have the latest revision of the piece in your hands; there's no reason to struggle through eighteen pages of galleys that have already been cut to ten by an editor. Read with a skeptical eye. If you like to make notes in the margin as you read, go ahead, but do not begin to mark facts systematically during this preliminary reading. Don't concentrate on the individual facts presented. Focus on the structure of the piece as a whole. This is the time to notice its varying degrees of rhetorical success and any obvious flaws in logic. Once you begin to check the facts, it becomes more difficult to concentrate on the writer's encompassing argument.

The first reading is not exactly fact-checking, but it may lead to a very useful understanding of the fact challenges posed by the piece. Your response to the piece will also help you anticipate where the editor may cut or revise it and where you should focus your efforts. The editor will almost certainly ask you what you thought of the piece, and you might as well start off your collaboration by indicating that you understand the big picture as well as the details you'll be discussing and perhaps arguing over later in the checking process.

What to Notice During a First Reading

• In a general way, do you find the piece credible and persuasive? Does the author seem well informed? If you yourself know little about the subject of the piece, you may want to skim other sources for articles and information before you try to make an assessment.

• How does the piece compare to other articles you may have read on the same topic? If you think that the issues have been addressed similarly elsewhere, you will want to confirm your recollection and then make sure the editor is aware of the precedent.

• Does the author's perspective seem notably biased or skewed? If so, you will need to be particularly diligent in fact-checking and should be prepared to go beyond the author's sources to get a more balanced perspective.

• Do any sections of the writing seem lifeless? They may need to be rewritten. You may want to check other areas of the piece before these dull ones, as they may change significantly.

Occasionally, flat writing can be a tip-off that an author is parroting someone else's ideas. When you contact the author after your second reading of the piece, ask that he or she identify sources for all unattributed information.

• Does any of the writing make questionable exaggerations? Hyperbolic assertions tend to disintegrate under checking scrutiny, so if the greater argument of the piece depends on suspiciously grand claims, beware. Plan to check these claims early so that the author and editor will have time to do the rewriting your checking may necessitate.

The Second Reading

During your second reading of the piece you will decide what needs to be checked. This time, take a colored pencil or pen, and as you read, underline statements of fact in the article. These should include any proper names; place-names; references to time, distance, date, season; physical descriptions; references to the sex of anyone described (names can be deceiving); quotations; and any arguments or narrative that depends on fact.

Determining What to Check in Nonfiction

In principle, determining what to check is straightforward. Take these sentences from John McPhee's 1968 book *The Pine Barrens.* Even before the checker has spoken to McPhee about his source material, she will have a general sense of what her checking will entail.

> If all the impounding reservoirs, storage reservoirs, and distribution reservoirs in the New York City water system were filled to capacity—from Neversink and Schoharie to the Croton basin and Central Park—the Pine Barrens aquifer would still contain thirty times as much water. So little of this water is used that it can be said to be untapped. Its constant temperature is fifty-four degrees, and in the language of the hydrological report on the Pine Barrens prepared in 1966 for the United States Geological Survey, "it can be expected to be bacterially sterile, odorless, clear; its chemical purity approaches that of uncontaminated rain-water or melted glacier ice."

Each of these sentences should be underlined in red, because each constitutes a statement of fact. In the first sentence the checker will need to confirm that there are indeed impounding reservoirs, storage reservoirs, and distribution reservoirs in the New York City water system and that Neversink, Schoharie, Croton basin, and Central Park are among those types of reservoirs in that system. The proper geographical names will have to be checked in a good atlas, *The Columbia Gazetteer of the World*, or a reputable state map. The quotation and details about the quality, temperature, and relative quantity of the Pine Barrens water must be checked against the survey McPhee mentions or against another reliable, preferably official source. Only one statement suggests speculation: "So little of this water is used that it can be said to be untapped." Perhaps this information comes from the survey, too, but if not, the checker will need to ask McPhee whether he has any sources that will support the assertion that the aquifer is effectively "untapped." If McPhee's argument is not wholly borne out by the sources he is able to provide or if his sources do not seem appropriately authoritative, the checker will ask him for the name of an expert on watersheds or find one through an environmental or governmental organization.

As far as these initial readings can suggest, McPhee's facts seem pretty hard. There is not much in the above excerpt to make the checker question the author's bias or argument. A sample from Joan Didion's beautifully written essay "Los Angeles Notebook," another nonfiction work, is slightly more worrying from the fact checker's point of view:

> A party at someone's house in Beverly Hills: a pink tent, two orchestras, a couple of French Communist directors in Cardin evening jackets, chili and hamburgers from Chasen's. The wife of an English actor sits at a table alone; she visits California rarely although her husband works here a good deal. An American who knows her slightly comes over to the table.
>
> "Marvelous to see you here," he says.

"Is it," she says.

"How long have you been here?"

"Too long."

She takes a fresh drink from a passing waiter and smiles at her husband, who is dancing.

The American tries again. He mentions her husband.

"I hear he's marvelous in this picture."

She looks at the American for the first time. When she finally speaks she enunciates every word very clearly. "He . . . is . . . also . . . a . . . fag," she says pleasantly.

As in the McPhee, a checker would underline every sentence to signify that these descriptions, characterizations, names, and quotations must be verified. The job facing the checker looks to be very different, however. With the help of the author's notes or perhaps by checking with another guest or the hosts, the checker will have to confirm that the party was actually in Beverly Hills, rather than in some adjacent neighborhood, and that there was a pink tent, orchestras (were there really two?), chili and hamburgers from Chasen's (if that is in fact how the name is spelled), and dancing. The checker would also want to confirm that the party included at least two French Communist directors who were wearing Cardin (this might require calls to their personal assistants), and that waiters brought round trays of drinks to the guests.

This paragraph presents an obvious peril if the Englishwoman and her husband the actor are identifiable to themselves or to others. They would probably take great offense at his being outed in this way. The checker should also consider how Didion heard this conversation, since the actor's wife is described as sitting alone at her table before being approached by the American man with whom she subsequently speaks. Alerted to these issues, the checker would discuss them with the author at the earliest possible opportunity so that the editor and legal counsel will be able to make a decision about whether, or how, to keep the anecdote in the piece.

When the Author Is an Expert

People who write about specialized subjects such as law, medicine, or science are often experts in their fields. For the most part, this does not mean that they can be considered the sole authority for their writing any more than the ordinary journalist can. Plan to check everything except those facts that only the author of the piece can confirm. If a doctor is describing her treatment of a patient, she can describe the treatment without having to provide evidence of every interaction included in the piece. (She should have made an agreement with the patient allowing the case to be discussed.) But beware of taking the author's word for too much. Perhaps because such expert writers are used to writing for academic publications, they often dumb down their reporting for an audience of laypeople. A little simplification is usually a good thing, but too much can be a disaster. In an article on the genetic sources of certain breast and reproductive organ cancers, a leading specialist failed to distinguish between two culpable genes, BRCA1 and BRCA2. Assuming that his lay readers wouldn't care for such nice distinctions, he referred to them as if they were a single gene. Fortunately, his fact checker read related medical studies and discovered why the difference between the genes was significant. He made a late change to correct references throughout the piece and prevented the dissemination of a misrepresentation.

Checking Reviews

Checkers underline and verify the facts in reviews of books, films, theater, dance, music, art exhibitions, and restaurants just as they would other nonfiction, being particularly vigilant when checking negative reviews. When checkers are not able to see a performance, exhibition, or movie for themselves, checking can be accomplished with the help of playbills, press kits, catalogs, and public relations people. The latter are often impatient and poorly informed, however, so it is preferable to use them as a last resort.

Book reviews can present interesting difficulties. In general, they are easy to check, because critics tend to write them using only the book under review and perhaps a few other printed sources. Problems often arise when the accuracy of the content of a nonfiction book is questionable. "Not every book reviewer . . . can or should plow through the original source material," Steve Brill, the founder and publisher of

Brill's Content, asserts. "But serious book reviews about serious books should try to do some or a lot of that. It's called reporting." This is a tall order, but there is some legal incentive for that degree of caution. If a book under review makes a libelous assertion that the reviewer then validates and publishes in advance of the publication of the book, the publisher of the review may be held liable for the disputed facts.

2

Source Material

After reading the piece through a couple of times, ask the editor of the piece if it is okay to call the author to discuss source material. Sometimes an editor will ask you to wait a day or so until the author has finished working on a new draft. You will need to consider the amount of time you think it will take you to check the piece. Is the proposed schedule for the piece realistic? If it is not feasible for you to do the work within the time allowed, can other checkers help you? If you think that waiting to talk to the author will still allow you enough time to check the piece before closing, fine. If not, you may need to persuade the editor or perhaps a superior or the department head to let you call right away.

When you call the author, consider whether she is familiar with the fact-checking process. Be as explicit as possible about what source material you want. It's a good idea to ask for more than you need. For instance, if the author has tape recordings of interviews but wants you to call the sources to go over the facts in their quotes, arrange to get the tapes as well as the sources' telephone numbers even though the tapes may seem unnecessary. You may find you need the tapes if you cannot reach a particular person or if the person denies saying something the author has written.

Tell the author exactly how you want the source material to be delivered. This, too, will depend on the length of time you have to complete the checking. All the sources for a short and straightforward piece might be sent by fax and e-mail. A longer, more complicated piece will almost always necessitate having more complex source material delivered to you by messenger, mail, or expedited service.

The Author's Responsibility to the Checker

Fact-checking protocol will vary from publication to publication, but in general, the author will provide sources of some kind to support all factual assertions. Sources can range from cocktail napkins scribbled with notes to tapes of interviews, transcripts, newspaper or magazine clippings, books, or other reference material, as well as videotapes. (If the tapes are foreign, you may have to allow extra time to have them reformatted for your video system.) You'll need the telephone numbers and possibly the e-mail addresses of the people she spoke to. The author should be prepared to help you find facts within the source material. She may want to talk you through the sources, highlight relevant passages in printed materials or transcripts, or annotate the most recent draft of the piece, citing the sources for each fact. Invariably, the author will not be able to provide adequate sources for every fact in the piece. You will have to discuss possible new sources for these facts and in many cases find them yourself. The author will arrange to be available to the checker to discuss sources and suggested changes and to answer any questions the checker may have. (For more on the author-checker relationship, see Chapter Three.)

Assessing Source Materials

Finding and evaluating sources is probably the most important work that fact checkers and writers do, because the quality of the source material used in writing and checking a piece determines the accuracy and breadth of the published work. With sources, the tasks of the checker and the author are more than compatible. They're identical. As a former head of research at *Vanity Fair* says, "A good fact checker is basically a good reporter." Finding good sources is like a treasure hunt. For many checkers it's the most enjoyable aspect of their work, and it's great training for writers.

Checkers provide essential insurance to writers (and to the publishers or broadcasters of the story) by making certain that the author's sources can reliably support her assertions. The checker has an advantage in that she or he can build upon the author's research. Media that are scrupulous about fact-checking make it a policy to insist that authors give their checkers all their source material, including printed material, tapes, transcripts, and notes. Checkers will use these for initial checking before going on to check more thoroughly.

Sometimes the amount of source material that authors send in can be daunting. If you have only a few days to check something complicated, the prospect of leafing through boxes of files, legal documents, and disorganized clips may seem so time-consuming that you would rather ignore the author's research altogether and see what you can check using the telephone and online resources. To save time, ask the author to annotate the piece and tell you, as precisely as he or she is able, where to find the supporting material. But never ignore the author's source material. Take the time to look at all of it at least once before you begin checking. Being familiar with the material before you begin to address individual facts can have unexpected rewards. One checker skimmed the jacket of a book the author had used as a source, only to realize later that the author had inadvertently "borrowed" some of the jacket copy when voicing his own opinion. General familiarity with the source forestalled plagiarism.

A good checker goes beyond the author's material to find additional support for the facts and thesis of the piece. The checker may come across information in new sources that casts doubt on the writer's facts and can use this new perspective as the basis for a suggested correction or to add a greater level of complexity to a piece that may be injudiciously skewed. As a senior researcher for the *Encyclopedia Britan-*

nica once put it, "Sometimes, in order to be more accurate, you have to be less certain."

Of course, not all sources are equally valuable. It takes experience, good judgment, and a little inside information to assess their merits. Human sources, newspapers, books, the Web, and Nexis and other online news sources each have their strengths and critical weaknesses. A good fact checker will keep them in mind.

Newspapers

Opponents of fact-checking are always quick to ask, "How can you say you're checking facts when you use sources that aren't fact-checked?" Most newspapers are not fact-checked. In their defense, many newspaper editors say they spot-check to keep their authors honest. Some copy editors check proper names and a limited number of other facts. Different sections of a paper may have different checking policies; an editor at one prominent weekly book review says that he spends somewhere between 25 and 35 percent of his time making sure that the reviews he runs are correct, from names and dates to quotations to plot summaries. He sounds just like a fact checker when he says, "However certain you are, look it up, because you *will* get it wrong."

Other factors may encourage accuracy at newspapers. Susan Shapiro, who studied fact-checking in three American news-weeklies, speculates that though they do not employ conventional fact checkers, newspapers have a better chance of being accurate than newsmagazines would if they were not checked. "Newsmagazine stories tend to be more synthetic, telescoping events over a greater span of time, analytic, colorfully written and therefore more ripe for inaccuracy than their daily print or broadcast counterparts. . . . Some would argue the editors and copy desks in daily newspapers, coupled with the greater beat specialization of bylined reporters, duplicate the functions of magazine fact checkers." On the other hand, another study found that almost a fifth of newspaper stories contained errors that were the result of editorial interference. One Canadian music critic had an experience typical of this kind of error: He worked with a copy editor who repeatedly changed his references to Beethoven's Eroica Symphony to the Erotica Symphony.

Historically, *The New York Times* has had a particularly high reputation for accuracy, but in 2000, the paper's executive editor reportedly decided that the rate of corrections—more than six per day—had become embarrassing. He called a meeting to address the problem. Reporters frequently misspelled names such as Stendhal and Madeleine Albright, but these were picayune errors compared to the incorrect facts underpinning stories on such serious subjects as the purported melting of the polar ice cap. Since the meeting, reporters at the paper say that standards have improved, but a glance at the corrections page shows that readers are still complaining. (The scandal over fabrications by *Times* reporter Jayson Blair, which broke in the spring of 2003, may have led to a certain hypervigilance among readers trolling for errors.) If the *Times* has accuracy problems, you can assume that other newspapers do, too. Among U.S. papers, the *Los Angeles Times* and *The Washington Post* are generally assumed to be about as accurate as the *Times*, but it may sometimes be true that a small paper will be a very reliable source for local news because of its proximity to events, the familiarity of the beat, and a high degree of accountability. Use your good judgment, but remain skeptical of papers whatever their reputation.

However their accuracy may vary, newspapers are invaluable to fact checkers, particularly when checking current news stories. The trick is to remember that they are fallible and never to rely on newspapers to check anything that you could check with a better source, such as a reliable reference book or a scholar. Most importantly, never use a newspaper to check the spelling of a name. There is always another way to get it right, and your odds are not good if you do not go beyond the paper. As always, don't rely on any one source exclusively to check any kind of fact. Cross-check with different sources whenever possible. Deirdre Casper, head of research at *Reader's Digest*, suggests using newspapers as a starting point from which you can pursue primary sources. If, however, you're stuck checking something from newspapers alone, try to get a sense of consensus among several good ones, making sure that they are not all getting their facts from one reporter's account.

If the author is depending too heavily upon a single newspaper source for information or an anecdote, suggest that he credit the source. Of course, if too much is borrowed from a single source, crediting the original won't solve the problem. The author has evidently done too little of her own reporting, and if there's time before the piece closes, she may have to do a bit more work. Quite possibly, however, that last-minute reporting will fall to the checker.

LexisNexis, Factiva, and Other Online News Databases

While many newspapers, magazines, wire services, television networks, and radio stations, both large and small, now have Web sites that can be searched independently, for most fact checkers the great advantage of using online subscriber services such as LexisNexis is the ability to search groups of publications for specific words, quotes, bylines, or subjects. LexisNexis's other services include finder files that can be used to locate people, addresses, and telephone numbers, as well as view driver's license and motor vehicle records. Company files allow you to access financial reports and to scan for companies with particular characteristics. LexisNexis also contains federal government information, including congressional transcripts and press releases. The Lexis part of the service focuses on the law and legal information; Nexis is devoted primarily to news and business documents.

Most checkers and journalists whose employers can afford to subscribe are addicted to Nexis. Its news content is no more accurate than the newspapers and other media that are reproduced in its files, so checking from it is potentially dangerous. (Nexis does have the advantage that the papers can append corrections to a piece they know contains an error. Unfortunately, the percentage of errors corrected this way is quite low.) Most research editors recommend that Nexis be used primarily as a first step, before moving on to primary sources. As in newspapers, the spellings of proper names on Nexis are particularly suspect, though the ability to search so many sources at once allows you to see how many times a name is spelled in a particular way. It can be fun to check on Nexis to see how many times a simple name such as Warren Buffett is misspelled.

Nexis is an ideal tool for certain checking tasks, if not for spelling. It's a good idea to search Nexis before beginning to check a piece, to see what other pieces have appeared on the same subject and how a story is covered elsewhere. This can give you a broader perspective on the story or it can reveal that the piece you are checking is alarmingly similar to something already published elsewhere. In the latter case, ask the author if she or he knows about the other story and discuss the overlap with the editor as soon as possible so that there is time for the author to do additional reporting or rewriting.

Very occasionally a checker may discover that the author has already published in another publication some part of the piece he or she was about to check. Usually this is a matter of foreign publication, but the checker ought to talk to the editor about the discovery immediately. Some authors are tempted to rework ideas or subjects that they've written about in the past, and it may be necessary to use a service such as Nexis to make sure that they do not plagiarize themselves.

The Web

Like newspapers and Nexis, the Web is invaluable but unreliable. Always go beyond it and find a good reference book or primary source. As Tina Kelley wrote in *The New York Times*, "On the World Wide Web, straight facts can be hard to find. After ploughing through dense and recalcitrant search engines that offer more sites than you can point a mouse at, after enduring delays, lost links and dead ends and arriving at a site that looks just right, Web surfers must deal with uncertainty: Is the information true, unbiased and free of hidden sales pitches?"

At worst, some Web sites are deliberately misleading or biased; more commonly, content is badly edited and out-of-date. However, the volume of information on the Web makes it an efficient way to get initial information on almost anything. You might use a search engine such as Google to find out where a particular scholar teaches. You might type in a phrase from an elusive quotation of poetry, and if you are lucky, you might find a facsimile page that has been scanned in at some distant library. You can also find information from foreign countries that may be difficult to access by telephone and Web sites for journals and newspapers that are not included in Nexis or the like. The Associated Press (AP) online photo archive might have a photograph of a riot the author is describing, or you might find a digital image of a painting that you can't find in any book. But don't trust the Web for the title of that painting, which you ought to be able to track down through a museum or library. Even official Web sites for institutions often contain misspellings and incorrect information, so you're always safer talking to or reading from an authoritative source.

Books

It's one thing to say that books are authoritative sources. It's quite another to find books that live up to that expectation. Reference books are fairly safe, although they vary in quality. *Books in Print*, for example, is not a particularly useful source for exact book titles or authors' names. It will list the book's publisher, though, and a good checker can call the publicity department to confirm name and title. *Who's Who* is also slightly suspect. The entries are compiled from responses mailed in by the subjects of the entries, and these are not fact-checked. But in general, reference books are edited with the knowledge that they will be used for fact-checking. Although they do contain errors, they are good sources when a primary source is not available. Consult two books if possible. If you find a conflict, go to a primary source rather than a third book. Sometimes the correct fact is elusive in print. Woody Allen's real name, for example, is spelled incorrectly in several sources.

When a checker tried to confirm it, only a call to Allen's biographer established the spelling definitively. (See Chapter Nine for specific recommended reference titles.)

Nonfiction trade books are another matter. As David Brock confessed several years after he'd published a biography of Hillary Clinton, "All authors of big nonfiction books face the arduous task of generating headlines to spur book sales. Too often, authors succumb to market pressures by trafficking in rumor, using unreliable sources, or embellishing their material, all in the service of hype and buzz. Publishing houses are notoriously lax in fact-checking. Books are rarely retracted or even corrected." In other words, some books may be even more dangerous to check from than newspapers. If the material at issue is potentially libelous, your publication may be protected from a libel suit if you can prove that you are merely echoing an assertion that is already in print elsewhere. But this does not hold true in every country and every situation (see more about this in Chapter Six), so you should discuss the risks involved in repeating libelous information with an attorney as well as the author and editor.

To assess the fact-checking value of nonfiction books, checkers can do several things. First, look for the copyright date of the book to make sure that the information it contains is not outdated or likely to have been supplanted. Is the book published by a reputable house? If either an index or a bibliography is missing, the book may be unsound. Use *Books in Print*, amazon.com, or an online library catalog to see what other books the author has written. Use the Internet to find out where he or she now works (a university position could be reassuring) and go to Nexis or a similar service to search for critical reviews of the book. Browse on Nexis or the Web and see what other books and articles have been published on the same subject by other people. The authors or their books might prove to be useful for cross-checking information. Occasionally you may work with an author who really is the only published expert in his field. You may find yourself in the peculiar situation of having to look in his or her previously published books to confirm facts for a future publication. In this situation you must be especially diligent in looking for any critical reviews of the earlier book and also in asking for the author's help in sharing his sources with you.

When a fact checker working on a piece about the Concorde supersonic jet realized that the author's source books were too dated to be useful, she went online and found a professor at an English university who was preparing to publish his own book on the Concorde. The professor was able to help the checker update the author's information. Initially the author was grateful, but after some discussion he said, "I feel a little upset that you know more than I do about this," and became angry. Had he been more skeptical of his source material before he began writing, the conflict would not have occurred.

Human Sources

It's difficult to predict what a particular human source will be like before you talk to him or her. In the context of fact-checking, people can be fallible, manipulative, impatient, fearful, painstaking, or honest, and checking with them directly requires diplomacy, tact, and a dash of cunning. However unpredictable human sources can be, checkers stand to learn the most about a subject and avoid the greatest number of errors when checking directly with a knowledgeable person. This usually takes place over the telephone, because for this purpose talking is the most efficient and nuanced means of communication available. A good writer will find authoritative human sources by the time the checker receives the piece, but the checker will almost certainly have to find additional sources. Determining who will make a good source depends upon common sense and sensitivity to both bias and conflicts of interest. Does the piece involve a lawsuit of some kind? Did the author speak to representatives from both sides? Are both positions represented in the piece? Are obviously biased sources matched by more objective voices? Has the author spoken to the best people in the field? Has he spoken to people who disagree with his thesis? Are their views represented in the piece? If not, the fact checker may have to supply these moderating voices. If a balanced article is not the goal, the checker should still discuss the imbalance with the editor to make sure he or she is aware of the author's bias.

For stories that involve businesses, you are almost always going to get more honest information from people at the top than from public relations people, for whom any indiscretion can be a threat to their jobs. Try the top executives first. Most people are interested enough in ensuring accuracy (or at least in protecting their version of events) that they will be willing to talk to you. Sometimes, of course, the top executive may not be the best source for every little fact about his or her business. Let's say a CEO is quoted talking about sales revenues. The author may have transcribed a quote correctly, and the executive may confirm the facts in the quote to you, but it is possible that he is not really an expert in the minutiae of his business operations. Be very specific about what you are trying to confirm and tactfully ask whether there is someone else who knows more about the details of the business.

Checking can eke out new facts from subjects whose lives might seem to have been exhausted by scrutiny. One checker spent three and a half hours fact-checking with Martin Scorsese for a magazine profile. In the course of their conversation, the checker went over some facts that a Scorsese biographer had included in her book, correcting a crucial misunderstanding. Ultimately that correction saved the magazine from embarrassment when the biographer asserted that the author of the piece had stolen her research.

Thorough checking directly with primary sources in this way can significantly enrich the writer's original reporting. As one former checker puts it, "Often when you call up a source the author's already spoken to, they'll open up to *you*. They're encouraged that you want their facts represented accurately. You're all on the side of the angels."

Finding the best sources for cross-checking can involve locating a scientist doing marginal research or tracking down the translator the author worked with while reporting the story, who may remember events that the author forgot to jot down in his notebook. You may need to find someone who worked with the victim of a murder, or you may need to speak to her doorman. The checker who has the ingenuity to find such sources to help round out a story or confirm facts that may otherwise have to be cut from the piece is doing an invaluable service for the author and the reader as well.

3

Due Decorum:
Working with Authors and Editors

The Delicate Balance

While the collaboration of fact checkers, authors, and editors should be a kind of holy trinity (with the author, like God, getting credit for the efforts of all three), working together can be a testy business. Julian Barnes, a novelist whose letters from London to *The New Yorker* were assiduously fact-checked, began a somewhat grudging encomium to checking by noting that checkers "bug you to hell and then they save your ass. They are also suspicious of generalization and rhetorical exaggeration and would prefer that last sentence to read: 'They bug you a quarter way to hell and on 17.34 percent of occasions they save your ass.'" Some of the best writers are terrible with facts and won't appreciate your hard work. In general, though, good writers appreciate good checking. Calvin Trillin, who says checkers have saved him from a number of embarrassments, observes, "People who are disparaging about checking are almost always the ones whose writing you can't trust. Of course checking can irritate, but it's worth it." He recalls a piece he wrote about Conrad Black's efforts to get into the House of Lords. When the checker was looking at the drawing intended to accompany the piece, which purported to show Black sitting on the House of Lords, she noticed that the artist had got the building wrong. The building on which Black was perched was actually the House of Commons. "It was an *incredible* save," Trillin says.

First-rate checking invariably improves writing, and most authors are ultimately grateful to checkers for making their pieces more accurate and better balanced. Earlier in the editorial process, however, many writers are defensive about the quality of their own research and are wary of having what they fear may be awkward changes inflicted upon their prose (or poetry, fiction, or illustration, for that matter). Editors, for their part, tend to be busy working on several things at once. They fear getting bogged down in pedantic arguments with checkers over minute changes. The checker must draw a fine line between being persistent and becoming obnoxious, between compromising and allowing substantial errors to slip past. Getting this line right is usually a matter of experience and temperament but may also require that you adjust your approach.

Veteran checkers say that the key to successful checking is to make the author feel that you're on her side. It's good if you can genuinely feel this way, too. After all, the author has done all the hard work of defining her subject, doing all the preliminary research, and, not least, writing. She may have had to limit the amount of research she did in order to get her piece written in time; you have the luxury of fact-checking intensively without ever shaping your findings into a coherent three-thousand-word argument. Even when you feel that the author could have done her research better than she did, you may still learn a lot from what she's accomplished.

How to Get Your Relationship with the Author Off to a Good Start and How to Spot Checking Problems Early

• Call the author as soon as your editor will allow. It may take a while for the author to gather up her source material and annotate a proof. Do whatever you can to get the process started immediately. If you are waiting for the author to return your initial call, go online or check Nexis and see what else has been published on the subject of your piece. Try to get a sense of what information and resources are available.

• Read the latest version of the piece before you call. Nothing is less confidence-inspiring than a checker who asks for source material to support facts that have been cut from a piece several revisions past.

• When you first talk to the author about the piece, praise whatever you like best about it, and be as specific as you can. Authors are starved for positive feedback, and it reassures them to know that you like the piece before you start meddling with their facts.

• Make sure that the author knows when the piece is scheduled to close. Find out if she will have enough time that day to work out the last crucial details in the piece with you and the editor. If she will be totally unavailable, talk to the editor of the piece, and perhaps to the managing editor, about changing the closing date. Closing a piece without the author is troublesome and can lead to changes being made to the piece without the author's approval—exactly what authors fear the most.

• Arrange to get source material from the author. Be specific about what you need and how you want it delivered. If an author hesitates about giving you notes or source material, be slightly wary. There might be nothing to worry about: Many newspaper journalists aren't accustomed to sharing their notes. Rodney Rothman's *New Yorker* story of November 27, 2000, "My Fake Job," contained a number of fact problems and failed to reveal that the author's mother was employed at an office that he described infiltrating. When Rothman was working with his fact checker, his attitude toward producing his source material could, in retrospect, have been a tip-off to his duplicity. At first he did not want to give up his notes on the grounds that the checker would think his jottings were "stupid." Then he claimed to have sent the checker the notes as well as recordings of his interviews, but he didn't—until the piece had actually been published.

• Try to make the author feel at ease. Do not let your questions take on the air of an interrogation. A calm and respectful manner will set the tenor of your future work together.

• Ask the author: "Is there anything in the piece you're particularly worried about my checking? How would you suggest I go about checking it so that it is least likely to cause problems?" The author may suggest a way to check the fact that you feel is insufficient. Discuss your concerns with the author and try to figure out another way to check it. If the sourcing remains tenuous, alert the editor. If it's a legally sensitive fact, you'll need to discuss your concerns with your publication's legal counsel.

• Ask the author: "Is there any source you spoke to whom you don't want me to call? Why?" The author may be afraid that a nervous source will become more skittish during a conversation with a fact checker, and will try to withdraw his consent to be quoted in the piece. (If the quote was obtained in good faith, it can be used even if the source announces that he wants to withdraw it, but it is understandable that an author would not want to get involved in such a conflict.) Sometimes writers fear the checkers will convey too much information about the content of the piece to a source and somehow jeopardize their reporting. You may decide that it is necessary for you to call a person despite the author's concerns. If so, you will have to persuade the author of your reasons before you do so and should be prepared to tell the author what you are going to ask the source.

• Make sure you understand the basis on which the author acquired her information. Was any of it off the record or on background? Is there any question that her sources knew she was going to write about them or quote them?

• Ask the author: "Do you have any personal connection to people or institutions that appear in the piece?" If so, she will almost certainly need to include an acknowledgment of this connection in the piece. At worst, the connection could be a source of bias in the reporting. The editor and possibly legal counsel will need to be apprised of the connection or any conflicts of interest immediately.

• Ask the author: "Did you make any deals with your sources in order to get better access? What were the exact terms of the deal? Did any of your sources insist upon quote approval?" Make sure the editor and possibly legal counsel are aware of any such arrangements.

• Establish a rough schedule of telephone or e-mail dates when you and the author will discuss the piece. This will give the author an early sense of how much you want her to be involved in the checking process. The more complicated the piece, the more time the author will have to set aside for fact-checking. Keeping to set dates will also make the author less likely to feel annoyed by an onslaught of unanticipated requests. You, in turn, will be able to use the arranged dates to better organize your own work schedule. Authors, like checkers, risk being perceived as demanding and intrusive. Formalizing your contact with dates will give each of you time to get your work done.

• If the piece is long and complicated, suggest that the author come into the office on the day the piece is scheduled to close. Having the author, editor, and fact checker together can really smooth the closing. The author can track down any stray facts using the source material she has sent you and can discuss any difficulties directly with the editor, you, and legal counsel. (If the author does plan to come in that day, bear in mind that you won't be able to get much checking done yourself while she's there, because you'll inevitably spend most of your time in discussions. Budget your time accordingly.)

Time Management

It's difficult to estimate how long it will take to check a piece. If it is underreported in some critical way (for example, if the author has failed to contact both sides in a legal dispute), you can be sure that checking it will take longer than usual, because you or the author will have to make new contacts and almost certainly insert new information. But even a well-researched, thoroughly reported piece can take longer than you might expect. You can anticipate delays if you will have to do any of the following:

• Listen to audiotapes if no transcripts are available.

• Reach sources in different time zones, particularly in less developed countries where there may be a limited number of international telephone lines available.

• Arrange to speak to jet-set VIP types.

• Get information from government sources.

• Acquire copies of original documents through the Freedom of Information Act (FOIA) or from attorneys or other sources.

Of course you don't want to cry wolf, but if you don't feel that the schedule allows you enough time to check a piece thoroughly, tell the head of your department, the editor, and the managing editor, *right away*. Perhaps the piece can be postponed, or perhaps you can get help from other checkers. Or perhaps, as many checkers have ruefully concluded, you can just work all night.

What to Check First

Each piece requires an individual approach. Before you do any checking, spend at least a few minutes thinking about what elements are likely to take the longest to confirm. You may want to ask the author's opinion on this, too. Sometimes it's best to study the author's written source material before getting on the phone. But if you know that you are going to need to ask for additional written source material (from an attorney, or as the result of a FOIA request), don't hesitate to request it—just making photocopies and sending the material via postal delivery could take longer than you have. If you suspect that you may have great difficulty reaching human sources, call them immediately. If they aren't available, try to set up telephone dates. Let them know when the piece is closing so that they will understand the urgency of your request. It may be sensible to tell them that the piece is closing before it really is so that you can be sure to hear from them in time. If the source is adversarial in some way, he or she may not get back to you until after the purported closing. (More about telephone checking in Chapter Four.)

Delegating Work to Other Checkers

If another checker is helping you on a big piece, think carefully about what you want to delegate. Consider your time limitations, his checking experience, and your own weaknesses as a checker. If, for example, you know that you have a tendency to leave the checking of proper names until the day of closing (checking names is perhaps your most important, if seemingly least challenging task), then this would be useful to delegate. The best way to choose what to delegate is to look at your sources. What groupings emerge? Could your helper check everything from written sources, while you do all the telephone checking? Your partner might concentrate on an entire section of the piece if the sources for it don't overlap with the sources for other sections you're working on.

When you're giving another checker work, remember that he's helping you out in a pinch, and show him gratitude and respect. Team checking can be fun if you can develop a little esprit de corps and keep your sense of humor intact. Be clear about the amount of time you expect the work to take and whether you'll need him to work after regular hours. Ask him to read the piece before you discuss the work. You may want to give him a choice of checking projects so that he doesn't feel that you're sloughing off the most tedious or most difficult tasks onto him. Don't leave any room for misunderstanding about what tasks you're assigning to the other checker. On a long piece, take a clean proof and mark the sections or individual facts you want him to check. In the margin, jot down the sources you suggest he use to confirm the facts. If you want the checker to call people, make sure to give him the correct phone numbers and remind him of any time differences. Make a photocopy of this proof for yourself. Indicate on your copy what your helper has finished checking so that nothing gets forgotten.

If you're the head checker, it's your responsibility to make sure that the entire piece gets checked to a good standard. Keep an eye out for any changes the author or editor might make to sections your helper is checking and add these new facts to your helper's list of tasks or take them on yourself. Discuss your helper's suggested changes with him before you go over the proof with the author. Make sure you understand and approve the sources the checker has used. If the changes are easily explained, it may be efficient for you to present them to the author along with your own corrections. If the justifications for your helper's changes are complicated, you may want to let him explain or defend them to the author himself. It can be hard to go to bat for someone else's corrections, which is one reason that it's good institutional policy for checkers to work directly with authors rather than relying upon editors to convey their concerns.

Presenting Your Queries and Corrections to the Author

It's important to review every change you want to make to a piece with the author before you make it. Very occasionally, an author may give a fact checker carte blanche to make whatever changes he thinks are advisable. Even when this is the case, make sure the author approves what you've done. As one checker-turned-writer puts it, "a pattern of communication with the writer protects the piece." The author should know the facts in her piece better than anyone and may know of some reason that your "fix" isn't accurate. The worst thing a checker can do is to introduce an error into a piece; authors are your best defense against this.

When authors gripe about fact-checking, their first complaint is that checkers will tell them that a fact is wrong but not tell them how to fix the problem. When you find a problem, suggest at least one fix. Try to disrupt the flow of the sentence or paragraph as little as possible. Your suggested fix should be, in the words of one columnist, "delicate and brief." Don't insist that every statement be qualified by wishy-washy words like "somewhat," "perhaps," "almost," or "maybe." Your first priority is accuracy, but your changes won't be approved by the author or the editor if they sound mealymouthed. (Rewriting sentences so that they'll be accurate and palatable to the author is one way fact-checking teaches great editing skills.)

Usually your negotiations with the author will take place over the telephone. Before you call, have your proof in front of you. The proof should be marked with your suggested fixes, as well as annotated with the sources you used to come to your conclusions. Note page numbers, when relevant, and perhaps jot down the sentence or two from the source that contradicts what the author has written. With this information, you'll be able to justify your changes and queries during the telephone call. It will also provide a lasting record of your research should you need to explain your choices after the piece has been published. Remember that the author presumably has good reason to believe that what she's written is correct. Your source may be fallible or misleading; be prepared to take into account the author's justifications for her original wording, which may be valid. If the author disputes your findings on a particular fact, you may need to check further using additional sources.

When you call, ask the author to have a proof in front of her. Discuss the facts in the piece in the order in which they appear. Begin the discussion of each new fact by telling her exactly where it appears and then reading the original sentence followed by the sentence as you would fix it. You might say something like, "Now, moving on to the top of the third paragraph on page five, where your sentence reads, 'Chef Anatole graduated from the Cordon Bleu while he was still in his teens,' I wondered if you would mind saying instead 'Anatole left the Cordon Bleu when he was only sixteen,' since according to page ninety-six of his biography, he dropped out in the middle of the second semester and never actually finished the program."

Possibly your author will agree. But perhaps she will reply that Anatole told her the biography was written by a hack and is riddled with errors. Perhaps she saw some sort of a Cordon Bleu document on the wall of Anatole's house in Provence. Clearly, you'll need to inquire further. Maybe your author will have Anatole's widow's telephone number; she might know. And the Cordon Bleu will probably have a record of its graduates that you can consult. Make a note of the author's suggestions on your proof and indicate to yourself that this fact, which you had considered checked, is still unconfirmed. You may end your conversation with the author feeling that suddenly you have a lot more to check than you had thought, but another way of looking at it is to acknowledge that as a result of your conversation, you are a lot closer to really getting the facts right.

Be careful not to check the author's opinion. Let's say she's a Washington insider. If the author writes that "George W. Bush is obsessed with golf," she's making a subjective judgment. You can imagine the consternation you'd provoke if you called the White House press office and tried to confirm the obsession. Alarm bells would start ringing; the PR people would worry that perhaps your author was implying that Bush was obsessed with golf *at the expense of his foreign policy*, and the next thing you'd know you'd get a blanket denial that Bush was obsessed, which would leave you in the position of having to make a change to a perfectly defensible characterization. Avoid this kind of overly literal checking. On the other hand, if after publication it turned out that Bush had never picked up a golf club in his life and was instead preoccupied by thoughts of croquet, you'd have an even more embarrassing problem on your hands. Deciding what to leave unchecked and deciding what to check require equal care.

Keep a good record of your negotiations with the author by taking notes on the proof you're working from. When the author agrees to your fix, mark it in some way that will be clear to you. If you negotiate a change that's different from but as acceptable as your fix, write it down exactly as you and the author have agreed. When you've finished talking to the author, give your changes to the editor. The proof you have been working on may be messy and confusing, so you'll probably want to copy your changes onto a clean proof. Be very careful not to miss any of the fixes and perhaps add a few words to explain subtle or complicated changes. If you transmit your changes to the editor via computer, make sure to keep a copy of what you've sent, as well as your notes from talking to the author, so that you have a paper trail you can use to retrace the checking process if necessary.

When You and the Author Don't Agree

Even if your source material is unimpeachable and your fix seems ideal, the author may not want to make a change. You may simply disagree about how precisely accurate the piece needs to be. Only experience and good judgment can help you decide when to compromise. If you've reached a stalemate, often the most diplomatic and time-efficient thing to say is, "Let's see what the editor thinks." Circle the contested fact on your proof for the editor, and in the margin write (or, if working on computer, insert into the text) a brief synopsis of your position and the author's. Then let the editor decide. If you feel the fact at issue is very significant, you can always bring it up again the next time you talk to the author. As a last resort, discuss your feelings with your department head or with your publication's legal counsel.

Leaving Facts "On Author"

The phrase "on author" is written on checking proofs at *The New Yorker* and some other magazines to let the editor know that a particular fact has not been verified by a fact checker. The checker is relying solely on the author's certainty that the fact is correct. Although the phrase may not be familiar in many editorial departments, in effect checkers everywhere do decide not to check certain facts.

"On author" should be reserved for trivial facts that for some good reason you can't confirm. If the fact is truly inconsequential and the author is confident that it is correct, you and the author can decide between yourselves to leave it "on author" and inform only the editor. Often "on author" is used for facts of which the author has some personal knowledge. Did the man standing behind the author in line at the polling station really have pink hair and a German accent? The author has no notes to support this statement, but you have to take her word for it, unless she knows someone else in the same line whom you could call for confirmation. Even if the man in line can recognize himself if he happens to read the piece, he's unlikely to be seriously miffed if his hair color is actually fuschia and he was born in Copenhagen.

Occasionally "on author" may also be used for more important facts when a trusted author is adamant that you not check something or when you determine that something is too risky to check. Let's say the mistress of a now-deceased famous man writes in her memoir that her lover had his own telephone next to the bed he shared with his wife, from which he called his mistress for intimate conversations while his wife was lying next to him. Since the famous man is dead, you can't ask him. And who else, besides his mistress (a somewhat biased source) would know? Only his wife, who at seventy-five is a social butterfly who heads a foundation in her husband's name. Before using "on author," try to imagine the consequences of not checking the fact. Weigh these consequences against the potential risks of calling a touchy source. In this instance, if you call the wife, you can anticipate that she would be motivated to deny the allegation, whether it is true or not. You would have to include her denial in the piece, which might interfere with the gossipy, first-person voice in which the story is written. She may be very upset about the prospect of her husband's mistress publishing an account of the affair and contact her lawyers in an effort to prevent publication. On the other hand, if you don't call her, she might do exactly the same thing after the piece appears in print. At that time she could add to her complaints that no one had attempted to contact her for confirmation. You're gambling either way. When the fact is significant, be certain to consult the editor, your department head, and legal counsel. This should be a group decision, because such decisions can have far-reaching consequences.

When Fact-Checking Becomes Research

In theory, fact-checking and research are different. Fact-checking verifies information that the author has provided.

Research finds new information for the author to use. In practice, fact checkers do a lot of research, particularly if they are good at their job and the authors that they work with see them as partners of a sort.

There are a few pitfalls to watch out for. If you find great written material that the author would like to include in the piece, ask another checker to do you the favor of checking that the quotation is verbatim. It's rare to get a long transcription exactly right. Do the same with quotations from human sources. It can be tempting to let yourself get away with conflations and omissions that you'd challenge in someone else's reporting. You may be very successful at getting new quotes. "Sources will sometimes be more open with a fact checker than they were when the author interviewed them," recalls one former checker. The danger is that if you begin to be perceived as a journalist rather than a checker, you may lose the trust, and the frankness, that sources often offer checkers.

The final pitfall is a psychological one. If you begin to help report a piece, you may stop being a partner with the author and become an adversary, carrying on a subdued battle for control of the story. You need to remember whose piece it is (and who is going to get the credit in the end). Learn when to back off, and reserve your authorial energy for your own writing.

Working Amicably with the Editor

Because editors are generally very busy, they want you, the fact checker, to do your job efficiently and promptly. They want you to get along with the author because they don't want to waste a lot of time listening to her complain about how annoying fact-checking is. They want you to write clever fixes so that you don't give them more editing work to do, and they want you to give them your changes as early as possible because they don't want to have to worry about fiddling around with a piece just before it closes. (This is, unfortunately, unavoidable, but hope springs eternal even in the jaded editor's heart.) The editor's relationship with the checker is less inherently fraught than that of the author and the checker, but even so, keeping the editor happy requires good manners, good humor, and diplomacy. Authors tend to come and go, but you'll probably work with the same editors again and again. It's worth earning their respect.

• When you first talk to the editor after you've been assigned a particular piece, ask what the status of the piece is. Some editors resist distributing stories they're working on until they feel that they've gotten the pieces into good shape. If the editor is a perfectionist, this could be much too late for you to begin your checking. Request that editors give you a copy—whatever its condition—right away.

• Ask the editor about whether or by how much the piece is expected to be cut or lengthened. Ask when the cuts or additions are expected. Will any particular section of the piece change very significantly? This information can help you decide where to begin your checking.

• Ask the editor's permission to contact the author. The editor may be waiting for the author to turn in a revision of the piece and may not want her disturbed until she produces it. Or he may know that she is flying back from Tibet and won't be sufficiently revived to speak to you until tomorrow afternoon. You may be able to do some preliminary checking before speaking to the author, of course, using the Internet and printed materials, but you'll need to talk to her as soon as possible to begin substantive work. The editor won't want to delay you but may have good reasons for asking you to wait before contacting the author.

• Ask the editor when your checking proofs are due. Coordinate this time with those dates you've arranged with the author.

• If the author asks you to send the latest version of a piece, ask the editor's permission before you do. The editor may want to discuss changes he's made to the piece with the author before she sees them.

• Don't make any changes to the piece without clearing them with the editor. Occasionally an editor may give you or the copy editor the authority to make changes without his or her approval. Even if this is the case, be sure to point them out to the editor as soon as you can.

• Giving editors your changes orally isn't acceptable. Always hand your changes in on the latest revision of the piece. (If you're putting your changes directly onto a story using a computer system, this may be self-evident.) Make sure to get your proof back from the editor after he's finished with it. You need to have a written record of your checking and suggested changes. If your editor is absentminded, make a photocopy for yourself before you hand in the proof.

• Give changes to the editor as early as you can, not in one lump immediately before closing. The editor will have to look very carefully at the passages you've changed, which will take time that he may have planned to spend otherwise.

• If you give an editor a proof marked with a change that you haven't cleared with the author, mark it so that the editor will know before making the change.

• Let the editor know about major problems of structure, argument, or reporting as soon as you discover them.

• Before you get behind schedule, discuss any difficulties you're having with the checking and alert the editor right away if you don't think you'll be able to finish the checking by the time the piece is scheduled to close.

When You and the Editor Don't Agree

When editors reject your fixes (which can happen even after the author agrees to them), you must decide whether it seems more reasonable to compromise or to fight for your change. The editor may convince you that the change isn't as necessary as you had originally thought. If you feel comfortable not making the change, write some indication of the discussion on your proof, and let the matter rest. But if the changes seem important to you, you don't have to give up at once. Discuss them again, perhaps when you hand in the next round of checking proofs. Stick to the issues and don't become emotional. Vehemence tends to be less persuasive than quiet, clear communication. If you can, use your sense of humor to lower any heat in the debate. Acknowledge the editor's reasons for resisting the change. You might say something like, "I can see why you think it's awkward to insert a reference to the journalist who originally broke this story. But if we don't mention her, it will look as if our author is borrowing her research and failing to give her any credit. We might end up looking bad." If the fact is significant and you feel the editor is being unreasonable in continuing to reject a change, discuss it with a superior editor and/or legal counsel.

Bear in mind that accuracy and ethical reporting may not be the editor's first priority for the piece. He or she may want the story to be as stylish and juicy as possible. A *Vanity Fair* checker encountered this attitude when working on a Gail Sheehy story about Hillary Clinton. Sheehy used a quotation that the transcript of her interview clearly indicated was "off the record." The checker argued that the quote should be omitted, but she couldn't convince Sheehy or the editors. They just didn't think being ethically upstanding was worth losing a great quote. If your editor railroads you on a serious matter, beware. Make sure you have written evidence that you've discussed the pertinent issues and suggested appropriate changes, even if the editor refuses to take many of them into account. Go to your department head, to a superior editor, or to legal counsel to discuss your worries as soon as the problem becomes evident. If they side with the editor, give up gracefully. In the end, how much you can influence the content of a piece depends on your publication's institutional standards. You have to alert the editors to potential problems, but they're the ones who must make the final decisions.

4

Checking Quotations and Talking to Sources

The *Jeffrey Masson v. Janet Malcolm* suit of the mid-1980s to the early '90s changed the way that quotations are fact-checked at certain publications and made people in the editing world reevaluate their quotation policies. In brief, Jeffrey Masson, a psychoanalyst and former projects director of the Sigmund Freud Archives, contested a number of quotations that the writer Janet Malcolm attributed to him in a long profile published in two parts by *The New Yorker* magazine in 1983 and in book form by Alfred A. Knopf as *In the Freud Archives* in 1984. Among other quotations, Masson contested one in which he compared himself to "an intellectual gigolo" and one stating that after Anna Freud's death he hoped to turn her house into "a place of sex, women, fun." In 1984 Masson sued for libel first under California law in the federal district court. The court granted the defendant's plea for summary judgment, which meant that the case couldn't be taken to trial. This was affirmed by the Ninth Circuit Court of

Appeals. In 1991 the U.S. Supreme Court, however, felt differently.

Considering five quotations that were not found on Malcolm's tape recordings of her interviews (she said that they had taken place during other conversations of which she had taken notes by hand), Justice Anthony Kennedy found that the style of Malcolm's article and the reputation of the magazine where the work was published would lead a reader to believe that the quotations were not a "rhetorical device" or a "paraphrase," but rather "nearly verbatim reports of statements made by the subject." The court admitted that there was no way to define exactly what might constitute acceptable editorial changes in grammar and syntax. Legally, these changes were irrelevant unless they created defamatory meaning. "Deliberate or reckless falsification that comprises actual malice [the standard that must be proven for the press to be found liable in a public figure libel action] turns upon words and punctuation only because words and punctuation express meaning. Meaning is the life of language. And . . . quotations may be a devastating instrument for conveying false meaning." If alterations to the quotations rendered statements defamatory, Kennedy continued, then "the words in the quotations might indeed be actionable." The court considered whether the words attributed to Masson materially altered the meaning of his statements. It found that some of the statements did appear to be altered materially, and that there was, in theory, evidence to support a finding of deliberate or reckless falsification, which allowed the case to go to trial. Two federal district court trials followed in 1993 and 1994; and the last one found, in favor of Malcolm and *The New Yorker*, that the disputed quotations were not libelous.

Several aspects of the *Masson v. Malcolm* case were relevant to fact-checking. One serious internal problem the trials revealed was that Janet Malcolm's editor at *The New Yorker*, Gardner Botsford, was also her husband. In retrospect, he seems to have lacked sufficient critical distance from his wife's work. He changed the location of one of Masson's monologues and reinstated the "sex, women, fun" quotation even after he discovered that the quotation was not on Malcolm's tape recordings. He said that he was satisfied by her notes. At trial, Malcolm could not present any handwritten notes, which appeared to have gone missing. (Masson argued that Malcolm never had taken handwritten notes.) Her only notes were typewritten summaries that supported three of the five quotations in question. (In 1995, Malcolm announced that her two-year-old granddaughter had found the notes for those three quotations in a bookcase at Malcolm's house in Massachusetts).

Fact-checking procedure at *The New Yorker* was considerably less stringent than it is now. Malcolm's fact checker, Nancy Franklin, gave a deposition for the federal district court and described her working method. It was *New Yorker* policy at the time that authors did not routinely give checkers their notes and that checkers did not listen to tapes. The reason for this, Franklin explained, was "to some extent a practical matter. There's not time. But even more important than that, it's not the job of the checkers to check quotes and to match what's on a tape up with what's in an article. . . . There are other ways of getting the information."

Franklin did check facts within the quotations.

Q: You have underlined under the words "The change in 'The Wizard of Oz' from black and white into color." Are you able to tell me why you underlined those lines?

A: Well, The Wizard of Oz is a real movie. It exists, and presumably it does or does not have a change from black and white into color, so that is something that you would have to check.

Q: You were checking that, but not whether Mr. Masson had in fact said that; is that correct?

A: That's correct.

Franklin also didn't check whether the events that Malcolm said had occurred at the restaurant Chez Panisse had actually occurred there. She did, however, call Masson and go over biographical facts with him. He later claimed that he had been upset by the number of errors in the facts Franklin asked him about and had asked her to let him review the parts of the story that quoted him or used information attributed to him. He said that Franklin had said she would get back to him, but never did. Franklin denied that he had made the request.

Since the scrutiny of quotations in the Masson v. Malcom

trials, most editors have asserted that they hold their publications to a high standard of accuracy for quotations. Checkers are now responsbile for confirming what was said, and in what context, and will usually see notes or transcripts and may even have tapes on hand. But at most publications, quotations are still far from being published "as spoken." In practice, says one writer, "it's a totally unregulated profession in which the rules can change from piece to piece and editor to editor. There's a tradition at some publications that the writing inside the quotes should be as good as the writing outside the quotes"— which is to say that if a quote needs to be cleaned up to make a story read better, it will be. In the November 1998 issue of *Brill's Content,* Katherine Rosman described an apparent contradiction in the quote policy at *Cosmopolitan.* Rosman found seven *Cosmopolitan* editors and staff who said "that during [Bonnie] Fuller's time as editor in chief, the magazine routinely fabricated anecdotes and invented named sources" in order to satisfy Fuller's ambitions for the stories. But Fuller asserted a more acceptable party line: "I'm not aware of it and if it happened, it's not something I would like or condone." As Rosman pointed out, *Cosmo* had a fact-checking department, but too often, quotes weren't checked if they were explicit or sensitive, particularly when source names were often changed anyway. High journalistic standards for quotations hardly seem to be required for many of the articles *Cosmo* publishes, but under Fuller readers apparently had no indication when the content wasn't reliable.

Cosmo's confused quote policy is an extreme example of a

more widespread problem with defining how far a quote can be rewritten by editors or authors. It's generally acceptable to eliminate repetition and correct grammar in quotations—we would all like to be more graceful on the page than we are in speech. But further changes risk altering the meaning of the quote. Magazines that publish legally sensitive writing and have a strict policy of not disguising sources must be especially careful about quoting. This doesn't mean that their authors don't clean up quotes or conflate conversations, but when there's a good checking department in place, there are more eyes scrutinizing these decisions to make sure that any alterations do not materially change the speaker's meaning.

Checking Facts Within Quotes

Remember that even if a quotation appears clearly in the author's notes or tapes, facts within the quotation may still need to be checked with independent sources. If a historian says, "It was New Year's morning, and as I stood on the banks of the Delaware River, I thought how far our country had come since George Washington crossed there on that same dawn in 1776," you'll want to check that the date, time, and names are correct (and, if you're really being careful, whether it is possible to stand on the banks of the river at the place where Washington crossed). Looking at a general but reliable source such as the *Columbia Encyclopedia*, and perhaps a history of the American Revolution, you would discover that it is generally reported that Washington crossed the Delaware on

Christmas night, not New Year's morning. What to do? Discuss your finding with the author. If the author wishes to be critical of the speaker's scholarship, she may want to leave the quotation as it is. To distance herself from the incorrect fact, she could insert a parenthetical correction following the quotation. It would be more generous, however, to give the historian a chance to correct the quotation. After all, it is difficult to be accurate when speaking off the cuff. In this case, the checker should call the source and politely suggest that he might have misspoken. Bear in mind that it is possible that your own written sources are wrong; perhaps the historian has found new evidence as to the correct hour of the crossing, if not its date. A discussion with the source might yield interesting new information for the piece or simply allow for a correction before the fact is printed. It would be a good idea to ask the historian for a second source you could speak to or consult to back up his assertion.

Sometimes you may judge that it's unnecessary to go beyond the speaker's recounting of a fact. When *Reader's Digest* published an interview with the actor Tom Hanks in which Hanks stated, "My father-in-law was tortured by the Communists, for crying out loud. And then he did everything he could to get to America. And you know what? He was nothing other than a bartender at the racetrack for 22 years." Although the checking department does check quotes and facts with quotes, it did not try to confirm this statement. They trusted Hanks to get it right. To an outsider, their decision is debatable. On one hand, Hanks presumably knows his father-in-law's life story and wouldn't want to misstate it. On the other, perhaps he has heard only a mythologized version of the past.

Assuming that there was a good reason for not confirming these facts directly with Hanks's father-in-law or another family member, it might make sense for the checker to ask Hanks if he was certain that he was telling the story accurately. The head of fact-checking at *Reader's Digest* says that in her experience, when people are questioned about their own anecdotes they are usually forthright about where they may have exaggerated or which facts they're not certain of. Double-checking with the speaker is an easy way to head off potential problems, especially when you are making a decision not to check certain facts.

A decision not to check facts in quotes should always take into account the reliability of the speaker (based on other facts you have checked up on), any possible motive that the speaker might have for making an incorrect statement, and how problematic it would be to check the fact independently. Finally, one must always ask, "What could happen if the fact is wrong?" A lawsuit would be the worst outcome, but to think only of legal liability sets a low standard for checking. Getting any facts wrong is embarrassing for the publication and diminishes its value in the eyes of its readers.

Relying on the Author's Notes to Check Quotations

Notes can be excellent source material or merely a starting point for checking. Whereas some reporters take notes carefully and legibly, others will jot down a few words on a water-ringed cocktail napkin. Depending upon the speaker and the substance of the quotation, even a cocktail napkin will sometimes do. But notes are selective, and they may deceive the author and you as to the context and completeness of a quotation. There are three questions to consider for every quotation: Did the speaker say roughly what the author quotes him or her as saying? Is the quotation in the correct context? And are the facts within the quotation accurate? It's usually a good idea to talk to the speaker even if the quotation appears in notes or transcripts. In conversation, a checker will often get a more complete sense of the speaker's full intended meaning than the notes can convey. For example, the author's notes might read: "caviar—osetra favorite. Serve at new year's party." From this the author might reasonably extrapolate that the speaker said, "Osetra's my favorite kind of caviar. We serve it at our firm's annual New Year's party." When the checker calls the speaker, she might discover that the notes are accurate but incomplete, and what has been left out changes the meaning of the quotation. The speaker might say that it would be more accurate to say, "Osetra's my favorite kind of caviar. But it's expensive, so for big parties like the one the firm gives at New Year's, the caviar we serve is a more ordinary kind." (When a quoted source provides new information to a checker, it is always worth taking a moment to think about whether the source might be attempting to spin or control the content of the piece to suit his or her own ends. In this example, the issue is the expense of the caviar. Might the source be trying to cover up his firm's extravagance? Perhaps they do serve the most expensive kind of caviar after all, but the speaker has suddenly realized that this information might appear to reflect badly on the firm's fiscal prudence.) Assuming that the changes seem to be legitimate, the checker has only to confirm that *osetra* is spelled correctly and that it is indeed more expensive than other kinds of caviar.

If a particular source or quotation is deemed too sensitive to check, the checker ought to indicate this to the editor and possibly to legal counsel so that the burden of deciding to leave a quote unconfirmed does not rest solely with the checker. As always, consider the possible result of not contacting a person whose quotation appears in the author's notes. It is generally a better idea to speak to him or her and face the consequences before publication.

Robert Walsh, who used to head the checking department at *Vanity Fair* and went on to become legal affairs editor there, says that the magazine is scrupulous about checking quotations. Notes, he says, "may be considered just as good as tapes. It has to do with the experience of the reporter. Some of our staff writers are wonderful note takers." There are certain occasions, such as when a writer accompanies an American delegation on a trip to the Middle East, when reporting can be done only with pen and paper. Walsh says that Dominick

Dunne's diary is another example of dependable reporting. In it, Dunne often records anecdotes told to him at dinner, and the checkers may rely only on his notes. Writers sometimes write down the answer to a question without recording the question itself. When this happens, Walsh says, "I do try to confirm with reporters what the context of a quotation was, and why they were unable to indicate it in their notes. In a certain way we're always anticipating possible problems."

Walsh says that *Vanity Fair* often uses ellipses to indicate where a quotation has been edited, but some magazines, such as *The New Yorker*, feel that they are aesthetically obtrusive and use as few as possible. They are obviously necessary if the quotation is from a written source, such as a letter, or has been published elsewhere. (Your publication's style will dictate whether to use the three-dot or three-dot and four-dot ellipses style.) Most magazines would probably admit that in practice they allow authors to cut phrases or even sentences out of quotes if the cuts don't alter the context or meaning of what the speaker is saying. Quotes from VIPs and politicians should be as close to verbatim as possible. Such sources will often have their own tape recordings of their interviews, so be scrupulous.

Relying on Tapes and Transcripts

Audiotapes of interviews can be a *wonderful source*. They offer excellent legal protection. In a trial, libel lawyer David Korzenik says, "the factual support for an article needs to be reproducible; tapes are better than notes." He adds, "Everyone thinks they've been misquoted. Most people would sue a mirror for what it shows them in the morning if they could. Most people hate the way they speak, and only if they're sophisticated do they understand what they've said." Tapes prevent scared or touchy sources from being able to deny that they've said something, and tapes will usually (but not always) clarify what was on or off the record. They are invaluable for high-risk investigative writing.

Tapes are unwieldy checking material, however. It can take a long time to listen to them, and few authors have the patience to jot down where on a tape a quote can be heard. Usually checkers will work with a combination of tapes and transcripts. They may appear to be problem-free sources, but problems do occur. If the author has made his own transcriptions from the tapes, he may have edited them as he transcribed them, writing down only what he thinks he may find useful for his writing. Ask the author whether the transcripts are word-for-word; spot-check them to confirm this for yourself, and listen to the tapes to confirm any legally worrisome quotes.

Professional transcripts aren't foolproof, either. Anyone who has worked with depositions knows the errors that can creep into a transcript when the transcriber is not an expert in the subject under discussion. When writer Michael Kelly relied on a professional transcript of his interview with William J. Bennett, Republican secretary of education, drug czar, and compiler of *The Book of Virtues*, for a *New Yorker* article, he used the transcript to quote Bennett as saying, "It's a real S&M kind of thing." Kelly's team of checkers, who were working on a tight schedule, checked the quotation against the transcript but did not feel they had time to check the original tape recording. Bennett disputed the quotation, and sure enough, the tape had recorded "It's a real us and them kind of thing." The magazine had to publish a correction.

Checking with Sources by Telephone

Phoning the source is always a good idea, even if you have notes or tapes. There are some things that you should always check directly with a source even if you feel you've got the quotations covered; most name spellings, for example, or personal information that might have been misunderstood or only partially reported by the author.

Get the author's permission before calling a source, and ask if there is anything the author would particularly like you to review with the source or anything you ought to be wary of. It's best to go through the author's notes, tapes, or transcripts before calling the source so that you can ask as few questions as possible over the phone, particularly on controversial issues. If the author hasn't given you much written material and you're going to be doing most of your checking by phone, it's still worth doing a little homework before you call anyone. Look up the subject on the Internet or in an encyclopedia to get some basic information. Though it is hard to believe, the art critic Hilton Kramer recalls a fact checker calling him with a question about Cubism; she said she thought it had something to do with Cuba. A little preliminary reading could have made that conversation go much more smoothly.

Before you call any sources, go through the piece and mark which quotations and facts to check with which people. The sources the author gives you may not alone be authoritative enough to confirm objective facts; after you've checked quotes with their speakers you may need to check the facts within the quotes with other sources you find on your own or in written materials. Talk to the author about how you intend to proceed so that she can give you her opinion about the bias of possible secondary sources.

When you call the source, give a brief description of fact-checking. Explain that you'll be asking seemingly disconnected questions about facts that have been pulled out of context. Many sources will say something like, "Wouldn't it be easier if you sent me a copy of what you're checking? I could read it and get back to you." Unless the author has made an explicit arrangement with this particular source, you'll have to say no, but make it clear that the call offers the source an opportunity to correct details of the piece over the phone.

Keep a record of your call, jotting down notes on the proof you're working on or on a pad you can keep as a record. Libel lawyer David Korzenik advises checking defensively; keep in mind that the source might sue your publication. You may need to provide evidence of the conversation should your work ever be scrutinized by lawyers. Korzenik warns, "If you don't have a record of that phone call existing, you have one less witness to testify to your good faith." Lawsuits are mercifully rare, but even under ordinary circumstances your notes will help you when you discuss your changes with the author and you need to remember exactly what a source told you.

Some checkers feel that phone conversations go better when they ask sources easy questions first and gradually work up to the more difficult ones. This sequence allows you to establish some rapport with the source before putting him or her on the defensive. Asking open-ended questions is helpful, too. If you ask, "How would you describe your relationship with your father?" you're likely to get the same answer the author did, because she or he probably asked the question that way, too. If, on the other hand, you say (mimicking the language you're trying to check), "Is it fair to say that you had a rotten relationship with your father?" the source is likely to balk and equivocate, even if that is exactly what he said in the first place. You do need to be diplomatic when talking to a source, but Korzenik says that as a lawyer, he's "increasingly less worried about revealing what's been written to a source. Usually it just helps bleed out potential problems."

Checking with the Source by Letter, Fax, or E-mail

Always try to contact a source by telephone before using written communication. Your copies of questions you've sent to sources can provide useful proof that you've made a good faith effort to contact them, but written queries have certain drawbacks. When corresponding with sources you don't have a chance to establish rapport or to gauge how best to work with them. You won't be able to make your tone or your questions more palatable to a nervous source. Worst of all, sources often give very limited responses to written questions, and you're stuck with having to accommodate those answers in the piece.

If it is impossible to communicate with your source except in writing:

• Check with the author and editor before sending a written query that is very long or that you anticipate may cause problems.

• Send queries out early in the checking process. If they're sent late, it could be argued that you didn't give your source sufficient time to reply.

• Always date your correspondence.

• Keep copies of your correspondence.

• Preface your queries with a brief explanation of the fact-checking process, give a deadline for a response, and encourage the recipient to call you to discuss your questions by phone rather than responding in writing.

• Consider how the order in which you present your questions may determine the response you receive.

On the Record, Off the Record, On Background, and Not for Attribution

In 1999, the Gannett Newspaper Division published its principles of ethical conduct, which can be found on the American Society of Newspaper Editors' Web site at www.asne.org. Gannett defined "on the record" as meaning that "statements may be quoted directly or indirectly and will be attributed." "For background" or "not for attribution" signaled an agreement that "the information may be used in the story but not attributed to the source." "Off the record" was defined as meaning that the information would not be used in the story unless it was obtained again from another source. Widespread confusion exists about the meaning of these terms, but Gannett's guidelines are sensible.

Fact checkers are often the only people involved in preparing a piece for publication who will listen to the author's tapes or read transcripts of interviews. They need to look out for mention of these terms and make sure that the author hasn't accidentally used material that he or she has agreed is "off the record," or attributed information or a quote to a source who has given the information "on background." Unfortunately, there are a lot of gray areas. Sources rarely say when they consider a conversation back "on the record," or when material *may* be attributed to them following comments that could *not*. The author may have a better sense of these transitions than a transcript or notes can convey. Discuss instances where the permission to use the information or quote is unclear, and make sure that the editor is aware of the issue. Whenever possible, clarify the status of the information with the source. Before calling the source, tell the author you wish to do so and ask him to agree to your discussing the intended status of the quotes. Sometimes asking about quotes will present the source with an opportunity to retract permission even if he or she granted it previously.

Anonymous Sources and Disguised Identities

Publications each have their own policies about the use of anonymous sources. In general, authors will tell fact checkers the identities of their sources so that checkers can do their work assessing the accuracy of the quotations and the value of the source. However, checkers can be subpoenaed to reveal the source's identity, so in certain cases it may be better for them not to know. (Lawyers giving legal advice on the piece, on the other hand, are protected.)

Checkers play an important role in ensuring the confidentiality of unnamed sources. It's the checker's responsibility to make sure that any description of the unnamed source that appears in the piece does not identify the source to associates, friends, or family. If a person is being written about without his or her knowledge or agreement, the identity must be disguised from that person as well as from anyone who might know him or her. (The author should indicate to the reader that certain personal details and names, if pseudonyms are used, are not authentic.) In addition to protecting the source or character as he or she appears on the page, the checker must be discreet about the identity when talking to other sources.

Look out for the improper use of anonymous sources. Authors occasionally create a false impression of consensus by attributing information, opinions, or quotations to several anonymous sources when in fact they have only one source. Alert the editor to places where the piece may be misleading about how many people were consulted. Checkers should also remember to corroborate facts given by unnamed sources. Because the sources cannot be held accountable for the information they give, checkers should back up the facts with another source whenever possible.

Dialect, Grammar, and Accents

When a quotation contains dialect words or indications of a speaker's accent or unconventional use of grammar, it's important that the checker consider whether they are correctly reported and whether the author has treated his sources equally in regard to these aspects of speech. This is not to say that an author cannot decide to quote one source or character speaking in dialect or with an accent when other figures in the piece do not, but such discrepancies may appear discriminatory. As usual, if the checker feels that the author is misrepresenting someone, he should discuss his concern with the author and subsequently with the editor.

Checking Diaries for Publication

Publishing previously unpublished diary entries presents particular difficulties. The simplest way to think of entries is to treat them as quotations—quotations that should be fact-checked, as far as possible, for accuracy and scrutinized for potential libel. When the diary writer is no longer alive, the checker may face difficulties of transcription and of identifying people named in the book. Find out whether the people mentioned in the entries are alive or dead and whether any particularly scandalous anecdotes the diarist tells about them have been recounted in any form elsewhere. You may be able to check anecdotes with people mentioned in the diaries if they are still living. There is bound to be disparity in people's memories of any event, however, so ask questions delicately and allow for reasonable differences in recollection. As always, you'll have to assess the reliability of your sources; diarists are not necessarily responsible reporters and may be exaggerating for their own titillation or to settle scores.

Even when the author of the diary is alive, supervising the publication, and accountable to his readers, copy editors, indexers, and fact checkers can face significant challenges. When Counterpoint published a recent edition of Ned Rorem's diaries, there was a flagrant mistake in the index. When the final hardcover edition of the book was printed, the index listed several references to *New York Times* critic Anthony Tommasini. One of the index entries for Tommasini referred to a description of Rorem's sexual liaison with "Tony the tiger"—whom the indexer had assumed was Tommasini. But "the tiger" was a different Tony. When Tommasini saw a copy of the book, he was outraged. To remedy the error Counterpoint was obliged to withdraw the book and cut out the relevant index page (fortunately the last page in the volume) and tip in a new one, a considerable bother and expense. Clearly, indexes are not always correct. One book editor admits that "indexes are notoriously rife with errors because they are the last part of a book that is compiled. Everyone thinks books are for the record and that journalism is for the day, but the fact is, given the time pressure, books are published a lot like articles." Be aware that indexes are usually not compiled by authors and may contain spelling and other errors or, in rare cases such as Tommasini's, misassignments of identity. You'd expect the diary of a living writer to be a reliable primary source. Clearly, it is wise to remain skeptical, especially if you are using a quotation or preparing to publish material that could be considered an invasion of privacy or defamatory.

Permissions and Fair Use of Quotations

Determining what constitutes fair use of copyrighted material is a task for legal counsel, rather than fact checkers, but checkers should be aware of the issues involved so that they can alert counsel to potential difficulties. In determining whether a long quotation constitutes copyright infringement, courts examine the purpose and character of the use of the material, how much of the copyrighted material was used, the nature of the use of the material, and any effect the infringement might have upon the market for the copyrighted work. Authors of book reviews and other critical writing can generally quote larger portions of text without fear of infringement; parodies or satires are usually safe, too.

It is better to be safe than sorry, and checkers should be aware that written permission from the copyright holder may be necessary to use quotations from material not in the public domain. The author should know where to apply for permission. If the author cannot identify the copyright holder, there are some obvious places to look. Copyright notices can be found in the first few pages of published books. ASCAP, BMI, and SESAC can provide copyright information for song lyrics and music via their telephone services and Web sites. (See listings under Recommended Sources at the end of this book.) In a pinch (and for a price), the U.S. Copyright Office will search its catalog, but be forewarned that not all copyrights are in their current catalog.

Quoting Letters

It is not uncommon for authors to quote from unpublished letters. Remember that the quotation must be verbatim. Unlike quotations delivered orally, there isn't any wiggle room. Make sure that there are no omissions or conflations of the text and that the date and context of the letter are correctly described. Look at the letter or a photocopy of it to confirm the author's transcription. If the letter is not in the public domain (ask your legal counsel about how to determine this), you will also have to obtain permission to quote from the letter if the author has not already given explicit permission. Copyright for an un-published letter is generally held by the author or his heirs, rather than the recipient of the letter, although the recipient owns the physical entity of the letter. Permission to publish part or all of the letter must be obtained from the letter's author (or her estate or the library collection that holds the letter).

5

Plagiarism and Fabrication

Defining Plagiarism

Defining plagiarism is always tricky, although most people have an intuitive recognition of when too much of another person's work has been used without correct attribution. For the purposes of fact-checking, the definition of plagiarism must be broad enough to cover a popular as well as legal understanding of the term. (Legally, plagiarism is addressed by the laws of copyright infringement and "fair use.") The Modern Language Association has a useful description of plagiarism. "To use another's ideas or expressions in your writing is to plagiarize. Plagiarism, then, constitutes intellectual theft. Strictly speaking, it is a moral and ethical offense rather than a legal one, since most instances of plagiarism fall outside the scope of copyright infringement, a legal offense.... Nonetheless, plagiarism often carries severe penalties...." To avoid charges of plagiarism, authors must cite their sources even when using their own words in paraphrase of the sources. Ideas must be attributed to their originators even if the originators' words are not used. Words spoken or written by other people must be attributed to them and enclosed in quotation marks.

A surprising number of successful writers, including historian and art critic Robert Hughes, National Public Radio (NPR) reporter Nina Totenberg, romance novelist Janet Dailey, and fiction writer David Leavitt have faced charges of plagiarism. (Leavitt was sued under British law for charges that he had, in effect, appropriated the life of Sir Stephen Spender—as chronicled in Spender's memoir—for the purposes of a novel. For more about checking fiction, see Chapter Seven.) Whereas some writers seem to have continued their careers without plagiarism accusations having real effect, others have lost their jobs and sunk into obscurity. Plagiarism is a serious charge that can have serious ramifications, even if, as is usually true, the issue never goes to court.

Of course, writers are targets for plagiarism as well as its perpetrators. Editors of literary journals occasionally receive submissions from obscure writers of poems that were in fact written by William Shakespeare. Most editors are able to identify these as hoaxes, but they have greater difficulty recognizing work by less familiar legitimate writers. The prizewinning poet Neal Bowers found that his poems (as well as those of Sharon Olds and others) were being plagiarized and published by a slippery impostor named David Jones. Bowers's book about his hunt for Jones, *Words for the Taking*, chronicles how difficult it was to stop Jones from publishing, even after Bowers had done as much as he could to inform likely editors of the hoax. This kind of fraud is fairly unusual, however, and fact checkers are unlikely to encounter it.

Professional writers are rarely intentional plagiarists, but the pressure of producing work in short order can make even a careful writer sloppy. Occasionally, a writer's work may be edited in such a way that quotation marks and attributions are cut from the text without the author's agreement, making the writer appear to plagiarize. And some authors seem oblivious to the good working methods that ethics demand. One of these, apparently, was Stephen Ambrose, who after a long and prolific career as a historian and biographer, was shown to have used sentences from other writers' work without quotation marks or attribution within the text (he did footnote his sources). He told David Kirkpatrick of *The New York Times*, "I wish I had put the quotation marks in, but I didn't." He added, "I am not out there stealing other people's writings. If I am writing up a passage and it is a story I want to tell and this story fits and a part of it is from other people's writing, I just type it up that way and put in a footnote. I just want to know where the hell it came from." This is exactly what writers should never do; they should never copy other people's words as if they were their own. But Ambrose, despite having a Ph.D. and many books to his credit, seemed to be unaware of the convention. (Interestingly, Ambrose's researcher is also his son, a relationship perhaps too close for the critical distance that might have helped save Ambrose from embarrassment. Just as Janet Malcolm should probably have had an editor who wasn't also her husband, Ambrose should probably have used a researcher—and ideally, a fact checker—who was not a relative.)

Plagiarism and Computers

The use of word processors and access to the Internet have made writers more susceptible to plagiarism. When writers cut and paste text into their writing from their notes or from material written by other people, it is very easy for the boundaries of authorship to be lost. In an interview with the *American Journalism Review,* the journalist Ruth Shalit explained how she had come to plagiarize (in one of the several pieces for which she has been accused of using other people's writing). "The mistake came from having somebody else's words on my screen and later conflating them with my own notes. That is always a bad idea. I'm [now] printing out all of my Nexis searches so somebody else's words are not up on my computer screen and I'm not toggling back and forth."

The Too-Good Memory

If having a flawed memory for one's sources is an obvious danger, so is having too good a memory for other people's ideas and phrases. Writers whose memories cling to felicitous prose may find themselves parroting other people's writing without realizing what they are doing. The only way to prevent these repetitions is for the checker to read as much of the author's source material as possible so that he will notice when phrases sound familiar. A familiar-sounding phrase can be researched on the Internet or on Nexis to identify any record of previous publication. Writers who are prone to borrowing other writers' work get reputations for doing so pretty quickly. It's helpful for checkers to discuss authors' writing habits. If you are about to check an author for the first time, ask a checker who has worked with him or her before about whether borrowing has been a problem in the past. The more you know about an author's typical treatment of facts, the better your chances of catching a problem before it goes to press.

Self-Plagiarism

Some writers can be guilty of what one could call "self-plagiarism," although as Alexander Lindey pointed out in his book *Plagiarism and Originality*, the term is a misnomer. "A man can't steal his umbrella or his own automobile. He *can* (though he may not) steal his own brainchild. If he takes a published work of his, alters it here and there, and puts it forward under a new title, he wrongs his first publisher, cheats the second, and swindles his readers. And if the original copyright is held by someone else, both he and his second publisher become liable for infringement."

Just as students are honor bound not to submit papers they have written for one class for another, writers must be careful that they don't tread on the same ground twice. This can be very difficult. If a writer develops a niche or a subject about which she writes repeatedly, she may find herself saying the same thing twice. After all, her opinion and the way she believes it is best expressed may not change from month to month or even year to year. Again, the plagiarism may be unintentional, and a scrupulous checker or editor can save the author from embarrassment by looking through the author's earlier work to see where overlaps appear. Of course, different editors will have a different sense of the extent it is acceptable for an author to repeat himself. If you find entire sentences repeated, you should suggest a change and mention the repetition to the editor so that he or she is aware of the author's habit, if indeed it is one.

How Fact Checkers Can Catch Plagiarism Before It Is Published

Assiduous fact checkers stand a uniquely good chance of discovering plagiarism and remedying it before going to press. This is because they alone of the editorial staff have the opportunity to become as familiar with the author's source material as the author is herself. Checkers should always look at the author's sources carefully and critically, and ask the author where her ideas—not just quotations—come from. Sources should then be compared word for word with the author's work. Overlaps in terminology and phrasing should be marked on the proof, and checkers should suggest substitutions that are further from the language of the source. All ideas and quotations must be attributed.

If a source is used repeatedly throughout the piece, it is not enough to cite the source once. The author's debt to the source needs to be indicated wherever the reader might believe that the information was the author's own. The attribution should ideally come before the information, but as long as the ownership of the idea or language is conveyed, the placement of attribution does not really matter. As always, checkers have to balance their obligation to help make the author's writing watertight with sensitivity to the author's prose style. A heavily annotated style may be appropriate for an academic audience, but the expectations for a popular news piece are different. Protect the author and yourself by indicating where you think attributions are necessary, but once the author adds some basic attributions, be prepared to compromise for the flow of the piece.

Use of the Internet and Nexis

Typically, the people most worried about plagiarism are professors, researchers, and teachers. For this market, Web sites and software programs now exist that can compare suspect writing samples with thousands of other texts. Fact checkers and editors worried about plagiarism can use Nexis and the Internet to see if they can find previous publications of bits of writing that seem familiar. Typing in specific terms and phrases may yield sources that the author has not told the checker about or is not aware of. It's a good way for the checker to familiarize himself with other writing on the author's subject, a key step in checking anything, whether or not plagiarism is a concern.

Checking for Plagiarism of Ideas

Assessing the originality of a writer's research or ideas is much more difficult than identifying sources for parroted language, and in most cases should probably only be attempted if the author makes claims for his originality that seem too good to be true. Checkers can start by researching the subject online and on Nexis. As a second step, checkers can access university or reference library catalogs online or directly and use subject searches to find books written on the author's subject. If time allows, a checker can consult the books for a better sense of how the subject has been covered elsewhere. If the subject concerns scientific research or research that claims to be groundbreaking, it may be wise for the checker to suggest to the editor that the checker do an informal peer review of the writing being checked. The manuscript could, in this special circumstance, be sent out to experts in the field (whom the checker could identify through recent publications on the topic or through a respected university). If time is short, the checker can telephone experts and discuss the issue. These experts stand a much better chance than the checker or editor of identifying possible instances of plagiarism in the piece.

Intentional Plagiarism

Intentional plagiarism is rare among professional writers. If in the course of fact-checking you find instances of plagiarism that appear to be the result of something worse than haste or oversight, discuss the problem with your editor and possibly with legal counsel. It is possible you won't find every instance of plagiarism in the piece, and what you don't know about could be worse than what you've already discovered. Your editor will talk to the author and make an informed decision as to whether publication is safe. As always, talk to your editor as soon as you can, to minimize the disruption caused by delayed or canceled publication.

Fabrication

When Patricia Smith, a winner of the American Society of Newspaper Editors Distinguished Writing Award for commentary and column writing and a Pulitzer Prize finalist, wrote her ultimate column for *The Boston Globe*, she admitted, "From time to time in my Metro column, to create the desired impact or slam home a salient point, I attributed quotes to people who didn't exist. I could give them names, even occupations, but I couldn't give them what they needed most—a heartbeat. As anyone who's ever touched a newspaper knows, that's one of the cardinal sins of journalism. Thou shalt not fabricate. No exceptions. No excuses."

Fabrication is not uncommon among writers; there are more than a few whose transgressions have caught the media's eye. Jayson Blair of *The New York Times*, Stephen Glass of *The New Republic*, Janet Cooke (the *Washington Post* reporter who won a Pulitzer Prize for her work on a nonexistent eight-year-old heroin addict), and far less egregiously, Rodney Rothman and Alistair Reid of *The New Yorker* have all included fictional elements in their nonfiction writing. It is natural for editors to come to trust writers they've worked with repeatedly and to give them the benefit of the doubt. Institutions that do not have fact checkers or do not insist that their checkers check assiduously tend to discover fabrication only after a pattern has emerged in many pieces by the same writer. Thorough fact-checking will usually expose the problem before a second, or perhaps just a first, suspect piece goes to press.

The Legacy of the New Journalism

Fabrication is nothing new, but recent patterns of fabrication may in part be a consequence of the New Journalism pioneered in the mid-1960s by writers including Truman Capote, Jimmy Breslin, Gay Talese, and Tom Wolfe. As Wolfe describes it, these writers used the novelistic techniques of scene-by-scene construction, realistic, fractured dialogue, a subjective point of view, and close attention to subtle indications of social status to transform reporting into something grander and more entertaining. Wolfe argued that this transformation was achieved without sacrificing accuracy, but one can sense the ambivalence toward facts in Gay Talese's statement that "the New Journalism . . . seeks a larger truth than is possible through the mere compilation of verifiable facts."

The New Journalism forced journalists to reconsider the primacy of objective fact. In his nonfiction novel *In Cold Blood*, Capote created dramatic effect through fictional devices such as the invention of scenes and conversations that he could only imagine based on what his sources had told him. Christopher Hanson of the University of Maryland writes, "Such reconstruction is now a standard device in nonfiction prose. Mainstream news organizations regularly reprint book excerpts containing reconstructed dialogue. The technique's cinematic qualities have made it irresistible. Bogus narrators likewise help the prosaic leap off the page and threaten for that reason to become regular fare." One could argue that the New Journalists' looseness with facts changed reporting standards for some writers, making fabrication seem both more acceptable and more necessary. Traditional reportage began to look dull when compared with the excitement offered by "fictionalized" nonfiction.

Fabrication's Warning Signs

If fabrication is a temptation for journalists because it offers the possibility of making reporting flashier, it is not surprising that the most obvious warning sign of fabrication is a story, anecdote, or quotation that strains credibility. Over and over again, when one looks at the reasons that readers or editors began to scrutinize the work of writers who were later proved to have plagiarized, credibility was the first test. When the ambitious young journalist Stephen Glass was exposed for having made up characters, stories, and quotations in numerous pieces he'd written for *The New Republic*, a former writer for the magazine told *The Washington Post*, "I always thought the stuff was too good to be true," because "every piece of his began with this really unbelievable sequence or anecdote." An editor at *The Boston Globe* felt the same sense of queasy disbelief when reading Patricia Smith's columns. "I recognized the same pattern. . . . Someone vaguely identified or not identified at all saying pretty incredible things." Other clues include the use of anonymous quotations, which one writer says is as dangerous as "giving a toddler a loaded gun."

Fact checkers who are allowed to do their work to a high standard will almost certainly catch fabrications before they go to press, although it is always possible that a checker and editor might trust an author too far and allow her too much leeway once or twice. Repeated fabrications would certainly be caught. Because Stephen Glass had been a fact checker himself at *The New Republic*, he seems to have been very good at finding excuses for why his supposed sources could not or should not be contacted by checkers. "A frequent tactic of his to elude fact checkers recontacting his source was to provide them with notes saying, 'This source is very nervous and specifically asks that you do not call him back,' even if there was a phone number," *New Republic* editor Charles

Lane told *The New York Times*. Glass also gave checkers fake notes and phone numbers and directed them to a Web site he'd created to provide evidence of a company that didn't actually exist. When checkers weren't able to confirm people's names on Nexis (a terrible idea in any case!), Glass showed notes in which he had the names spelled out with little dashes between the letters to indicate that he had checked them himself. Glass's example proves that when fact-checking from notes, making telephone calls to check basic information with the people quoted is still necessary. If *The New Republic*'s checkers had persevered, Glass's pattern of fabrication would have been exposed much earlier. As it was, it took only one person, Adam Penenberg—then a writer at Forbes Digital Tool—who was willing to check one of Glass's published pieces thoroughly to find out that it was riddled with holes.

In the case of Patricia Smith's nonexistent sources, Smith first claimed that the people she quoted in her columns were too marginal to be traced; they didn't have telephones. Later, when editors at the *Globe* tried to track down some of her sources with computer databases, they could not find a number of them. Eventually Smith resigned after confessing to fabricating sources for four columns. According to *Brill's Content*, fifty-two of her columns were subsequently placed in doubt. Like most newspapers, *The Boston Globe* had no fact checkers on staff. Once Smith's editors decided to scrutinize her work, they uncovered her fabrications very quickly. They might have been able to prevent the problem entirely if they had had a policy of insisting that writers provide phone numbers for sources or tapes of interviews. An occasional spot check would have revealed the problem. It isn't realistic to expect that a large daily paper should fact check every piece thoroughly, but as Smith's example shows, that extent of care wouldn't have been necessary. Her fabrications weren't as elaborately concealed as Stephen Glass's because they didn't need to be—she did not anticipate any fact-checking—but in the end both fabrications were crude enough to be uncovered easily.

"Innocent" Fabricators

Some authors—perhaps followers of the New Journalism—just don't see a clear line between writing fiction and nonfiction. They may fabricate some elements in a nonfiction piece that is otherwise well reported and think nothing of it. Their lack of awareness that this type of fabrication is taboo is what makes them "innocent." (British journalists seem to be particularly susceptible to this kind of innocent fabrication.) They simply don't understand what the fuss is about as long as their narrative embroidery makes for a good story.

One writer who was publishing an excerpt of his book about the settling of the West had used a historical society book about one region's pioneers as a source. The writer had taken family names from the book and proceeded to make up family histories for the real, though deceased, people. He provided the book he'd used for the names to the fact checker, which effectively gave the checker evidence of the facts of the real family histories from which his account had strayed. He was quite unrepentant when the checker pointed out the differences between the source and the author's retelling. The author had not fabricated facts throughout the piece. The problem was isolated. Such writers, though not suited to the hard fact requirements of newspaper reporting, probably do not deserve to be blackballed for their little fictions. The greatest danger they pose is to their fact checkers, who are responsible for discovering and correcting the fabrications.

When you're faced with an author who makes things up, you must, of course, discuss the problem with your editor as soon as possible. But don't overreact. What is important is that through careful fact-checking you've discovered the error. If the editor doesn't feel that the author has irrevocably betrayed her trust and deserves to have his piece killed, your next step will be to remedy the fabrication. You must report the facts accurately, using the sources you have, and perhaps go a bit further. In this example, you might find out if anyone with the family names you are concerned with still lives in the area. Get their telephone numbers and ask them to tell you about the family history for themselves. Original research is not the primary task of the fact checker, but making the piece accurate *is*. Once you have reliable facts, suggest substitutions for the author's fabrications that are in keeping with his prose style and fit, as nearly as possible, into the text as the author originally wrote it. You may feel tempted to rewrite much more of the piece than is strictly necessary, but even though you have borrowed the reporter's role, you are really just there to make sure nothing incorrect goes into print. If you don't have time to do original reporting for the piece and the author will not do it, suggest that the fabricated passage be cut.

6

Libel

Good checkers believe that all facts should be treated as if they were equally important. The publication of defamatory facts or visual images can give rise to a libel suit, however. If the facts are found to be incorrect and published with a degree of negligence or "actual malice" that meets the adjudicating state's requirements for libel of that particular plaintiff, damages can ensue. Some facts, then, need especially attentive checking.

The costs of fighting a libel suit are significant. George Freeman, assistant general counsel for *The New York Times*, says when publishers lose, awards for damages often exceed a million dollars. "Punitive damages get reversed and lowered on appeal, but they can end up in the many millions. About two-thirds to three-quarters of libel cases are lost by the media at trial. The same percentage are reversed on appeal. But by that time—five years or more, probably—the legal fees alone will run into the millions." When the Philip Morris Corporation sued the ABC television network for libel over a 1994

ABC report alleging that nicotine was intentionally added to cigarettes, ABC, which was by no means clearly in the wrong, decided to settle the case before going to court. They issued an apology for one statement and agreed to pay legal fees, which had already amounted to $15 million.

Carol Burnett's 1976 libel suit against *The National Enquirer* did go to court, even after the *Enquirer* published a retraction. Although Burnett's initial $1.6 million award (which was lowered on appeal) was far smaller than Philip Morris's legal fees, it was a substantial victory for a public figure. The *Enquirer* had implied that Burnett had drunk too much at a French restaurant in Washington, D.C., and had "become boisterous," eventually arguing with Henry Kissinger and "disturbing other guests." The *Enquirer* simply didn't have the facts to back up its story. According to Alex Beam of *The Atlantic Monthly*, "The case had a plethora of bad facts. In a deposition a Florida-based editor of the *Enquirer* said that he distrusted the source of the original report and had rewritten the report himself. A reporter testified that he had tried to fact check the item one hour before deadline and failed. Two of the restaurant's employees came forward and said they had told *Enquirer* reporters that Burnett hadn't been drunk at all." Under scrutiny, it was clear that the *Enquirer* editors had reason to believe that the story was flawed and decided to publish anyway.

Preventing a libel suit in the first place with thorough fact-checking is clearly the more cost-efficient option. Fortunately, good checking can do a lot to protect a publication from liability under libel law. Not only is truth always a defense against libel, but the very process of fact-checking, even when it fails to eliminate inaccuracy, can be a safeguard against liability.

Defining Libel

This discussion of libel will focus on its implications for fact-checking and will pass over aspects of the law that are less relevant to it. It is not intended to be a comprehensive guide to libel law, which varies in its particulars from state to state. Checkers need to be aware of the rudiments of libel law to the extent that they can alert their publication's lawyers when they encounter material that may be defamatory. Readers who are interested in more complete discussions of the subject might begin by looking at the concise but thorough discussions in *The Associated Press Stylebook and Briefing on Media Law* or *The First Amendment Handbook*, edited by Jane E. Kirtley and published by the Reporters Committee for Freedom of the Press, 1999. (The latter is available free online at www.rcfp.org/handbook.)

Different states define libel differently, but libel is broadly understood as published material that is defamatory, injuring a professional or personal reputation and causing damage to social or professional standing.

Who Can Sue

The law divides libel plaintiffs into public officials, public figures, and private figures. Again, courts differ in their definition of these categories of plaintiffs. In general, in order to collect damages, public officials and public figures have to prove that the defendant has acted with "actual malice," meaning a reckless disregard for the truth, a high standard that is often difficult for plaintiffs to prove. Private figures in most states have to meet a lower standard, proving only that the defendant was negligent. But in some states they may be subjected to a higher standard, as in New York, where they must be able to demonstrate that the press acted with "gross irresponsibility." It is best to be conservative when making assumptions about whether a potential plaintiff will have to meet the actual malice standard or a lower one. "It's very hard to predict if someone is a public figure for a particular purpose," says Gregory Welch, an attorney who has done prepublication reading for many magazines and newspapers. "I myself don't rely on assumptions about who is or isn't a public figure."

It isn't just individuals who can sue for libel. In certain states, small groups of people may be able to sue, although class action libel suits and libel suits by governments are not allowed. According to the Libel Defense Resource Center, the most common plaintiff is a corporation. Corporations are not necessarily considered public figures, though, a fact that indicates the subtlety of legal distinctions among types of plaintiffs.

All plaintiffs have to prove that they are identifiable in the libelous material. If their identities are in some way disguised, this must be done so fully that they are not identifiable to any readers. "You only need one person other than the plaintiff and the defendant to recognize the plaintiff," says media lawyer Jeffrey Blum. The best way to think about this is to ask whether the person would be identifiable to someone who knew them.

What Is Defamatory

Definitions of what is considered defamatory vary from state to state. To describe someone as homosexual, for example, is considered defamatory in some states but not in others. When checking, be wary of descriptions of criminal activity, facts about people's sexual activities, drug or alcohol use, or behavior that could be construed as socially unacceptable or unprofessional. Kevin Goering, a media lawyer at Coudert Brothers, says a good rule of thumb is "If it's something you wouldn't want to have said about you, it's probably defamatory."

To be actionable, the defamatory statement must also be false. Goering says, "You can't be sued if the statement is true except in very rare exceptions—for example, the intentional infliction of emotional distress. In some states, the public disclosure of intimate private facts could be a basis for an invasion of privacy case."

Photographs, captions, headlines, illustrations, and even poetry and fiction can contain defamatory material. In 1991, a young woman named Kimberly Bryson from southern Illinois launched a libel suit against News America Publications, Inc., which had published an issue of *Seventeen* magazine that contained a fiction story titled "Bryson." The character Bryson was described as "a slut," and Bryson argued that she was represented as being sexually promiscuous. The Illinois Supreme Court found that "the fact that the author used the plaintiff's actual name makes it reasonable that third persons would interpret the story as referring to the plaintiff, despite the fictional label. In addition, the setting of the story, the events described therein, and the identification of the writer as a native of southern Illinois all lead to a reasonable conclusion that third persons familiar with both the plaintiff and the defendant would understand the story as referring to the plaintiff." Although the defendant argued that the description of "Bryson" as "a slut" was opinion, which generally cannot be a basis for a libel suit, the court found that the statement was not protected under the First Amendment because it could be reasonably interpreted as stating actual facts. (Please see particular advice for checking these materials in Chapter Seven, Checking Fiction and Poetry, and Chapter Eight, Special Fact-Checking.)

Parroting defamatory statements, even in the form of accurate quotations, can give rise to charges of libel. It is known as "the rule against repetition." As attorney David Korzenik says, "If you quote something defamatory you're deemed to embrace it as your own. If you really need to quote someone and you can't verify what's being said, you need to tell the reader that there's no support for that statement. You want to have it pretty heavy-handedly clear that you are distant from the speaker. If you say that X is a rumor, it may reduce damages but it doesn't protect you against liability." Altering quotes may also lead to a charge of defamation if the speaker feels that the altered quote is false and defamatory, though it is important to note that altering quotations is legally permissible as long as doing so does not materially change their meaning. (For further discussion of this subject, see Chapter Four, Checking Quotations and Talking to Sources.)

Actual Malice

Libel plaintiffs who are public officials or public figures must prove that defendants published the libelous material with actual malice. The term is often misunderstood. The current legal understanding of actual malice dates from 1964, when the Supreme Court considered the case of *The New York Times v. Sullivan*. The case, which was first heard in the Alabama State Circuit Court, involved an advertisement placed in *The New York Times* by the Committee to Defend Martin Luther King and the Struggle for Freedom in the South. The advertisement described acts of harassment and intimidation of Dr. King and civil rights protesters by Alabama police. The descriptions were subsequently shown to contain some inaccuracies. Sullivan, who was then public safety commissioner in Montgomery, Alabama, sued the *Times* for libel (although he was not named in the ad). Under Alabama law, the *Times* was responsible for proving the truth of the allegedly libelous statements, and injury to the plaintiff was assumed if any of the statements could not be proven accurate. The Alabama jury had decided in favor of Sullivan and awarded him the half million dollars in damages he had sought.

When the U.S. Supreme Court reversed the decision, Associate Justice William Brennan wrote that the Constitution protected the press when writing about public officials regardless of whether what was written was true. "A rule compelling the critic of official conduct to guarantee the truth of all his factual assertions—and to do so on pain of libel judgments virtually unlimited in amount—leads to . . . self censorship. . . . Would-be critics of official conduct may be deterred from voicing their criticism, even though it is believed to be true and even if it is in fact true, because of doubt whether it can be proved in court or fear of the expense of having to do so." Brennan stated that in order to recover damages, a public official would have to prove that the allegedly libelous statements were published with actual malice, which he defined as "knowledge that it was false or with reckless disregard of whether it was false or not."

Following *The New York Times v. Sullivan*, damages in libel suits would no longer turn on whether the press could prove the truth of what had been written about public officials in their public capacities. Rather, after 1964 the public official was obliged to prove that the press had known or had strong reason to believe that what was being said was incorrect at the time of publication. (In 1967, the Supreme Court said that plaintiffs who were public figures would have to prove actual malice just as public officials did.) Plaintiffs have to provide a high standard of proof to meet the requirements for actual malice. The high standard protects the freedom of the press. Brennan argued that without this protection, fear of libel damages might dissuade the press from the kind of critical discussion of the public actions of public officials that the Constitution intended to foster.

A second case important to the fact checker's role in preventing libel damages is *Herbert v. Lando*. Herbert was a retired army officer who was the subject of a *60 Minutes* segment, produced by Lando, on CBS television. The broadcast was critical of Herbert, who had accused superior officers in Vietnam of covering up war crimes. Herbert sued for libel. As a public figure, he was obliged to prove actual malice. To meet the requirement that the plaintiff prove that prior to the broadcast the defendant had reckless disregard for the accuracy of the material or knew that it was false, Herbert demanded that the defendant provide information about the editorial process and the state of mind of those involved in the publication. The defendants refused to respond on the grounds that they were protected from these inquiries by the First Amendment. The Supreme Court found that the First Amendment gave the press no such protective privilege. It was already difficult for plaintiffs to prove actual malice. An editorial privilege would have made it nearly impossible.

When the court rejected CBS's attempt in *Herbert v. Lando*

to create an editorial process privilege, it made clear that plaintiffs could request that the defendant provide information that spoke to the defendant's state of mind as to the accuracy of the piece. David Korzenik says, "When the standard is actual malice, the trial is about the editorial process." Plaintiffs would certainly try to use evidence about the fact-checking process to determine the defendant's state of mind. Fact checkers who have worked on material that is the subject of an actual malice libel suit can expect to give a deposition and could be named as defendants. Their work and methods would certainly be examined by the plaintiff's counsel. There are a number of ways that checkers can help prevent the plaintiff's counsel from using their work against the defendant.

The Fact-Checking Process as a Safeguard Against Liability

Checkers want to make sure that every fact is correct before publication, and so they should. Because truth is always a defense against libel, having the facts right can make all the difference to the outcome of a suit. (It may often—though not always—prevent one from being filed.) It is always wise to be especially scrupulous about fact-checking when the story is sensitive, says Gregory Welch. "If things that aren't actionable are wrong it makes the piece look sloppy." But in the case of actual malice, inaccuracies are allowable if they are not published or written with actual malice, that is, strong intimations or knowledge of the inaccuracy of the facts prior to publication. "The best fact checker in the world can spend weeks on a piece and there will still be a mistake," says Jeffrey Blum, a partner at the Los Angeles office of Davis Wright Tremaine who specializes in the First Amendment and in prepublication reviewing for newspaper clients. "The First Amendment explicitly permits falsity." In general, it is the diligence of the entire editorial process that's ultimately on trial, and fact-checking can be what in legal terms would be called "affirmative evidence of lack of actual malice." "We've won cases because of fact-checking," says Blum. "The fact that a piece was fact-checked was compelling in dismissing libel claims."

In a libel action, fact-checking material and notes will be very carefully examined by the plaintiff's lawyers. In a suit by a private figure, who will probably have to meet only the standard of negligence, the plaintiff's counsel will hope to find evidence of some departure from a theoretical standard of fact-checking. For the much higher standard required by an actual malice suit, lawyers would probably look for evidence that the checker, author, or editor had been aware of factual problems with the piece and that the piece had been allowed to go to print without these problems being resolved. In theory, if fact-checking produced serious doubt as to the veracity of a statement and the statement was published despite those doubts being known to the author and publisher, the publication might be found guilty of actual malice. Gregory Welch warns, "If a publication doesn't fact check, it may be in greater danger of getting the facts wrong, perhaps dangerously so. However, if you are checking and you learn that something's false and you ignore it, then you're going to get in trouble."

David Korzenik says, "The process of fact-checking, in my view, should be conducted as if you have a reasonable juror looking over your shoulder while you check. The factual support for an article needs to be reproducible. You don't need to be overly cautious, but being able to demonstrate responsible checking will ultimately protect you. Checking method, however, is important. It's important to keep records of whom you've spoken to by telephone, for example. If you're talking to a sensitive source, you may want to get someone else to listen in on calls if it may end in one person's recollection opposing the other's." It's a good idea to use the margins of your proof to jot down notes about your phone conversations and the titles or names of sources you've used when checking specific facts.

The Problem with Memorandums

Whereas written notes will help provide evidence of the steps the checker has taken to ensure the accuracy of the piece, certain written communications can be dangerous if they have to be turned over to a plaintiff's attorneys in a libel suit. "Plaintiff's lawyers are very adept at taking everything in writing and turning it against the writer or the publisher. Notes are not always helpful to the defendant. Journalism is like sausage.

The end product is fine but you don't want to watch it being made," Kevin Goering says.

A memorandum was central to the issue of actual malice in the case of *Tavoulareas v. Washington Post Co.* William Tavoulareas, the president of Mobil Oil, sued *The Washington Post* for libel after the newspaper published articles suggesting that he had used his position to set his son up in business. A *Post* copy editor had written a memo, which was admitted as evidence, describing the story, before publication, as a "withered peanut in an 84-inch gilded shell." She had stated that she found it "impossible to believe" that Tavoulareas had set his son up in business as the article described. Because there was no evidence that the newspaper had addressed the copy editor's concerns or changed the story in response to them, the memo was used as evidence of actual malice.

"The fact that you've prepared a memo can be evidence of a lack of negligence," Kevin Goering believes. "If you didn't have a memo it could prove negligence. However, if the person responsible for publishing the text didn't address the concerns of the memo, that would be negligent. If you're going to memorialize what the problems are, you ought to memorialize the solutions to the problems, too." Korzenik agrees: "If you write a memo saying we're worried about this or that, you need to annotate it with your solutions. You want to express your concern in a way that makes it remediable. Say what needs to happen. A memo reflecting general doubt about a writer or an article is like a stick of dynamite. Try not to put unfocused or irremediable concerns on paper. Discuss your worries orally." (A checker's conversation with the publication's lawyer is usually protected.)

From the perspective of the fact checker, a memo can be very helpful if there has been difficulty in conversation in getting an author or editor to respond to serious factual concerns. (There may be an element of self-protection in writing a memo. Even when publication of a problematic piece doesn't result in a lawsuit, errors in the piece or controversy may lead to an informal internal investigation of how the piece was verified.) The process of writing the memo may help you to distill your argument and express it more clearly, and the recipient will be better able to focus on the elements of the problem. Written concerns of this kind can be helpful to the checking process, but as Korzenik and Goering have stressed, they should be followed by a response, documented in some way, that shows that the concerns were thoughtfully addressed before publication.

Foreign Libel Law

"Foreign libel law is relevant to United States publication because if even one copy of a book or magazine is distributed somewhere else in the world, and the content is deemed to have violated the rights of someone who might not even be a local citizen, a local court might try to exercise jurisdiction over the publisher and author," says Kevin Goering. Without exception, the laws of foreign countries are not as protective of authors as U.S. laws are. (Damages and legal costs, however, tend to be much less.)

Boris Berezovsky, a politician and businessman, and Nikolai Glouchkov, the managing director of Aeroflot, were described in a *Forbes* magazine article as "criminals on an outrageous scale." *Forbes* is based in New York, and the two men are Russian citizens. Nevertheless, the British House of Lords decided that the pair's personal and business connections to the United Kingdom made them eligible to sue under U.K. law, although neither was a British citizen, and *Forbes*'s British distribution was negligible. The decision by the House of Lords, made in the spring of 2000, led to talk of "libel tourists," who in theory might sue for libel in whatever country had laws most sympathetic to them. In 2003, the dispute was resolved when *Forbes* admitted it could not prove what the court claimed *Forbes* had said about the Russians. *Forbes* agreed to correct the material on its Web site.

The Internet may also encourage libel tourists. Jurisdiction over material available over the Internet is still being debated. In *Gutnick v. Dow Jones & Co., Inc.*, an Australian sued Dow Jones for an article that was available in Australia via the Internet. Gutnick claimed that the article implied he was guilty of money laundering and tax evasion. Dow Jones asserted that the state of New Jersey should have jurisdiction over the case because it was there that the article was loaded onto Dow Jones's server. An Australian court ruled that Gutnick could sue in Australia. Plaintiffs often win libel suits in Australia (and libel suits are common) because the law grants the press little protection for freedom of expression. The allegedly libelous statement is presumed false unless the press can prove otherwise. Recently, the press has been offered some protection. In 1997, *Lange v. Australian Broadcasting Corporation* extended a qualified privilege for statements about public figures and public officials in the context of governmental and political matters of public interest, under the conditions that the publisher had made appropriate attempts to verify the defamatory material, including requesting and publishing a response from the defamed figure (in other words, requiring good fact-checking). The privilege does not provide much protection for the press—certainly not as much as the U.S. actual malice standard does—so it is not surprising that Gutnick would choose to argue his claim there.

The Gutnick case may make it possible for Internet libel cases to be prosecuted nearly anywhere in the world. As yet, however, U.S. publishers are most concerned about the libel laws in the United Kingdom, because that is where American publishers have the most exposure. Until a few years ago, libel law in the United Kingdom was like that in the United States prior to the 1964 Supreme Court decision in *New York Times v. Sullivan*. In 1999, in the case of *Reynolds v. Times Newspapers Limited*, the House of Lords developed a privilege that depends upon whether the public has an interest in a subject and a right to know about it, and whether the press has a corresponding duty to report on it. The allegedly libelous story must meet a balancing test consisting of ten factors, including the urgency and timing of the piece, the source of the information included in the piece, and the steps taken to verify the information. The privilege is evolving as it is being applied in more cases, but as yet the balancing test makes it very difficult to predict whether the privilege will actually protect the publisher in a specific case.

Libel laws in certain other Anglophone countries may also be relevant to U.S. publications. In Canada, a qualified privilege for political figures is emerging, but the privilege doesn't go nearly as far in protecting the press as *New York Times v. Sullivan* did. Scotland and Ireland have their own libel laws and procedures. Scottish libel law differs only slightly from English law, but in Ireland the process is even more disadvantageous to publishers. Procedurally, it is very difficult to defend a libel case. There is almost no pretrial discovery, which means that defendants know very little about what they will face when plaintiffs present their cases. Libel law in Ireland is sometimes referred to as "trial by ambush." If your publication distributes there, and you are working on a sensitive piece involving possible defamation of Irish figures, beware.

7

Checking Fiction and Poetry

Whereas checkers of nonfiction try to hunt down any fictional elements that may have slipped in, checkers of poetry and fiction look out for anything that might be fact. Fiction and poetry present the same opportunities for libel as nonfiction, and it could be argued that writers of these forms are less sensitive to the dangers of blending fact and fiction than are journalists and reporters. Fact-checking fiction and poetry can be as interesting, and as risky, as checking nonfiction.

Suggesting and making factual changes to poetry and fiction requires particular delicacy. As one checker put it, "It's always a question of how much you're going to screw up their language." A great checker will suggest changes that are as minimal as possible and suit the style and formal qualities of the piece. However subtle they may be, checkers of poetry and fiction should expect to face resistance from their authors. Many fiction writers and poets feel that fact-checking is unnecessary. The novelist and scholar Frederick Busch parted company with an editor who tried to be too scrupulous with facts in Busch's novel, which he'd based on events in Herman Melville's life. Busch argues that "in most scholarly research, and in the digging out and reporting of news, *fact* means *true*. In the writing of fiction, *fact* and *truth* are less easy to reconcile." This sounds reasonable, and, indeed, it's best to fact check fiction and poetry with a light yet careful hand, but fact checkers can do an enormous service to writers and poets by checking objective facts. Not only can they fend off defamation suits, they can forestall the more quotidian damage that occurs when readers notice that a writer they trust has committed an error. Unfortunately for authors, most fiction and poetry is not checked much further than the spelling of proper names. Checkers who've worked on fiction and poetry know the gaffes that writers often commit—and how grateful the authors are when they have the opportunity to correct them before going to press.

As always, deciding what needs checking is the most important part of the job. Real-world facts that appear in fiction and poetry must be verified exactly as they would be in nonfiction, and invented facts, such as invented proper names, may need to be checked to make sure that they don't correspond too closely to real-world names and facts. Most authors sign contracts that assert that their fictions are not based in fact. In practice, however, many underestimate the care they should take when blending fact and fiction. It is only when a fact checker begins to ask them in detail about the sources of their characters, settings, and events that authors will provide clues to potential problems.

Real People and Fictional Characters

When characters in a poem or piece of fiction are based on real people, the checker must ensure that the real people are not identifiable to themselves or to others. Be especially careful when a character's personality or actions are presented as unethical, incompetent, irresponsible, or criminal. Giving the character an invented name is usually an insufficient disguise. Other facts must also be changed to prevent readers from associating the character with the person. These facts will vary from piece to piece but might include location and profession. Checkers should alert legal counsel and editors to the connection between real people and characters so that counsel can assess whether any part of the characterization could be found to be defamatory. Careful masking of certain pertinent facts can help protect the author from liability.

When Real Names Appear in Fiction and Poetry

When a checker first speaks to the author of a piece of fiction or poetry, he should ask the author whether any of the names are those of real people. The checking treatment will depend somewhat on the extent to which facts about the person in the piece are verifiable or imaginary (imagined elements must be presented as fantasy and not fact), and whether the characterization of actions could be construed as offensive.

As when checking a nonfiction piece, in almost every case the checker should contact the person named to confirm the spelling of the name and any other facts. This will also give the checker the opportunity to make certain that the named person knows about the impending publication of the piece. Of course, any checker would admit that appropriate protocol varies from piece to piece and author to author. When *Esquire* publishes David Sedaris's fiction, in which his family and friends appear, the head of the magazine's research department says, "We like to make sure that he's mentioned to everyone that they're in the piece." They would not feel the need to call up these people to confirm their name spellings or other facts, but they would ask Sedaris if he was less than 100 percent certain about anything. Sedaris has earned their trust, but with a writer whom they didn't know as well they would make the calls. Regardless of the author's reputation, checkers should always be alert for certain red flags. If the person is depicted as unethical, incompetent, irresponsible, or criminal, or if there is a possibility of a violation of his privacy, the checker should be sure to discuss the issues with the editor and legal counsel to avoid a lawsuit.

When a story or poem concerns a well-known person, the issues are much the same, although the checking procedure is different, because it is unlikely that the checker would need to contact him or her directly. (Libel law's differentiation between public and private figures might give the author more latitude.) In 1997 the poet Edward Field ran into problems when his poem "My Sister the Queen" was being prepared for publication in *The New Yorker* magazine. The poem depicted Queen Elizabeth II as cruelly preventing her sister Princess Margaret from marrying her true love, Captain Peter Townsend. The poem blurred fantasy and fact in a way that made it unclear whether Field was imagining details of the story or stating them as fact. The fact checkers consulted biographies of the royal family and found different reasons that the marriage never occurred. Field, for his part, argued that his poem echoed what British tabloids had written about the affair. Tabloid reporting is gossipy and unreliable, and *The New Yorker*'s poetry editor decided not to publish the poem on the grounds that it could be misconstrued as "accurate." Field, who had had a poem dropped by *The Atlantic Monthly* after his description of pigeon mating was disputed by his editor there, was outraged. To his mind, poetry is a kind of fiction, and fiction does not need to be held to a high standard for accuracy. But fiction, like non-fiction, can lead to libel. Would the royals have sued? Probably not. From the checking perspective, however, the ethical concerns remain the same.

The Potential for Libel

Just because an author thinks she's given a fictional name to a character doesn't mean that there isn't a real person with the same name, and if the real person's life matches the character's in other details, such as the city he inhabits, or the company where he works, or his profession, the coincidence could result in unintentional libel. Fact checkers must ensure that there can be no confusion between the character and any real person by checking that no one with the character's name lives in the named location or shares other (checkable) characteristics. Checkers begin their searches by looking up the names of residents of a particular area using telephone directories, calling directory information, or using Web search engines. Invented company names are checked in the same way to ensure that no real company with the same name exists.

When an Author Borrows Characters from Another Author's Work

When an author borrows characters, text, or plot from another writer's work and uses them in his own fiction, there may be danger of liability for plagiarism or copyright infringement, even if the author's intent was to satirize or otherwise comment on the original while creating a work wholly his own. Issues of fair use and public domain can be complicated, so if you encounter overlaps between the work you are checking and previously published work, you should speak to an attorney.

Fiction and Poetry Set in a Specific Historical Period

When *Harper's* magazine was preparing to publish a fiction piece containing facts about the German dirigible the *Hindenberg*, the checker had to find obscure information about the airship's various decks. She discovered a museum in Germany that had the data she needed, and says that ultimately, "we had to make changes, because there are a lot of *Hindenberg* freaks out there who know the facts." Checking poetry and fiction that is set in the past often requires greater creativity than checking nonfiction pieces on similar subjects. Fiction writers may have taken their information from sources less reliable than those a journalist would typically use, so checking may be less a matter of retracing the writer's steps than of researching the topic for the first time.

Fiction that incorporates historical events must be checked so that descriptions of the event correspond, as much as possible, with reliable accounts. Looking at trustworthy histories is an obvious start, but if particular details are elusive, checkers may find it more efficient to talk to a university professor who specializes in the period, to a museum curator, or to a historical society staff member. A personal response from an expert is often the best source. Experts can tell whether an account of an event is in keeping with what they know, even if they cannot confirm every single fact included in the description. Their sense of the general credibility of the description may be enough confirmation for a piece of fiction or poetry, though it might be insufficient for checking a nonfiction work. Similarly, when an author uses a historical figure as a character in fiction or poetry, checkers should allow the author some freedom to invent aspects of his character while preventing the publication of anything that contradicts established historical fact. Biographies are the obvious source for facts, but biographers or historians are again the best sources for this kind of checking.

Locations: Real Places and Fictional Places

Every week on National Public Radio, Garrison Keillor broadcasts tales about the private lives of the residents of Lake Wobegon, Minnesota. Of course, there's no real town called Lake Wobegon, which means that Keillor doesn't have to worry about whether there is a real Pastor Ingqvist who might be offended by his alter ego's behavior, and when Keillor says, "It's snowing in Lake Wobegon," radio listeners don't worry about where the storm is headed. All this would be different if Keillor set his stories in St. Paul. Each time Keillor invented a new character, he'd have to worry that a real person of the same name existed in St. Paul, and the weather would have to conform to local forecasts. Whether an author uses a real or invented location makes a tremendous difference to how checkers treat other facts in the story or poem.

Checkers should ask authors whether the named geographical locations of their stories or fiction are real or invented. If the author believes she's invented the place-name, checkers should use a good gazetteer and an atlas to check that there is no existing real location with which the invented one could be confused. If such confusion is possible, the checker should tell the author so that she can decide whether to invent another name (which must also be checked) or whether to leave the "real" name as it is and check other facts accordingly.

If the place-name is real, any fact about that place should be correct even though the story or poem is fictional. When

Russell Banks set a short story in upstate New York, fact checkers at *Esquire* had to confirm that the real hospital and restaurants he referred to were named and described accurately. On a more subtle level, they also had to make certain that the way his fictional characters were behaving at the hospital didn't malign the hospital's reputation. (Of course, the full names of any characters said to be living in a real place would be checked against telephone books or other sources to make sure there was no overlap between fact and fiction, particularly if the characters were shown to behave in an objectionable way.)

If a character eats lunch at a bandstand, the checker must make sure that there is in fact a bandstand in the town and that the author's description of it is accurate. (Is it Victorian, derelict, modern? Does it stand on the banks of a weed-choked pond?) Good sources for information of this kind are guidebooks, local historical societies, museums, and chambers of commerce. The Internet may be helpful as a first step, but always try to check with a second, human source, as Web sites can be misleading. A few small towns, for example, have created spoof Web sites for themselves containing photographs of geographical features, such as lakes, that do not exist.

Some authors are sloppy when they describe the distances between real places. If a character is driving from Spokane to Seattle, Washington, the time the author describes the trip as taking must be checked, unless it is a drive the author makes regularly and he or she attests to the time. An atlas will provide the distance in miles, from which the approximate time can be extrapolated. If the route described is mountainous or follows a tortuous coastline, mileage might not be a good indicator of the time the drive would take. In that case, a call to the Automobile Association of America or a local chamber of commerce or town hall might yield a better answer.

Flora and Fauna

When the novelist Alice Adams wrote a story set in her hometown of Chapel Hill, North Carolina, she described the roses in bloom there in the month of May. But when her checker called the botanical gardens, he found that this was nearly impossible. Roses just don't bloom there that early. The checker found several flowers that Adams could correctly describe as blooming in May and offered the author a choice, and the piece was corrected. Authors may fear that checking will mar their prose or poetry, but in this instance, as in most, checking helped the author to make her writing more specific and interesting.

Checking poetry and fiction often requires research into horticultural facts and facts about animals, including behavior and physical features. These facts are not hard to confirm. There are many excellent reference books on these subjects (see Chapter Nine, Checking Resources), but experts at zoos, aquariums, breeders' associations and other animal-interest organizations, horticultural societies, botanical gardens, and universities can provide help when you need more information than your reference books contain.

Objects

Real things that are described in poetry and fiction sometimes need to be checked against authoritative sources to make sure that the author has described them accurately. Proper names and trademarks must of course be checked. More interestingly, you might encounter questions about whether an object existed, as described, at a particular date in the past. For example, was a specific make and model of car available at the start of the Great Depression? How many seats did that model have? If the car was, in fact, a two-seater and your author has four people traveling comfortably in it, there is a problem.

Descriptions of art and architecture are fairly common in fiction and poetry, and they need careful checking. Obviously, names, dates, and attributions should be checked, but so should references to the content or composition of the work. Is it really Lincoln Cathedral that features "crazy vaulting"? How many women can be seen at work in Vermeer's painting *The Little Street*? Perhaps because authors tend to dig these images out of their fond memories of the works, rather than looking at the works as they write, their renderings are often partial or incorrect. In some cases of flawed recollection, the author and editor might decide that the flaw was interesting as an accurate depiction of the author's mind. In general, however, these errors should be corrected before sharp-eyed readers notice the mistakes and write furious and self-righteous letters of complaint.

8

Special Fact-Checking

The front page of *The New York Observer* carried a three-column-wide drawing that the caption identifies as depicting Bill Clinton flanked by campaign contributor Denise Rich and her daughter, Ilona Rich, a fashion designer. Ilona is shown wearing her "Bo-peep" dress and hat. The story continues onto another page, where it is accompanied by photographs of the Rich family and Ilona's clothes. From these, it's clear that the girl drawn on the front page in the "Bo-peep" outfit isn't Ilona Rich at all, but a model wearing one of Ilona's designs. Perhaps the person who wrote the front-page caption did not see the photographs. Possibly the front-page illustrator was given incorrect information about whom, exactly, he was drawing. However the mistake occurred, it was a fact-checking disaster. It could have been avoided if just one person had looked at the illustration, photographs, and captions with an eye on the facts.

Readers pay more attention to photographs and illustrations, and their accompanying captions, than they do to text. When the subject of a photograph is misidentified, or when the art conflicts with the text it illustrates, readers notice right away. Visual images really stand out; fact checkers need to be particularly careful when working with them. Unfortunately, checkers can find it difficult to get reliable information on visual images and may need to exercise some ingenuity to be certain that images are identified as they should be and used appropriately.

Checking Drawings, Cartoons, and Paintings

Checkers look at drawn or painted images, such as cartoons or illustrations, in an unusual way. As when checking text, the crucial thing is to determine whether, or how, the image deviates from verisimilitude. Not all art has to conform to reality, but it's the checker's job to establish where the difference lies. When checking a drawing, they will scrutinize the way a man's jacket buttons (the buttons should be on his right). They'll wonder whether the drawing is being printed backward, meaning that everything—such as jacket buttons—will be reversed. Checkers notice whether people, objects, places, buildings, maps, and animals look in drawings approximately as they do in life. Personal recollection isn't enough. If you need to check how many legs a mosquito has or confirm the outline of a continent, you must look it up in a reliable reference book. Misrepresentation isn't just a matter of looks. If a rock star is caricatured as smiling brightly while clutching a martini glass, the checker will want to make sure that the star has not been on the wagon for the past decade. If an image looks oddly like the work of another artist, copyright infringement could be a concern. Sometimes a drawing may be based on a photograph or another work of art; it's important that the original artist receive credit. When there's any doubt about the source of an image, call the artist and ask.

Checking Photography

Photography presents a particular set of problems. The first question to ask is whether the photograph is of what it purports to be. You might think this would be obvious, but mistakes abound. With thorough fact-checking, these are often caught before they get into print. Photo editors tend to get their information about the content of a photograph from the photo agency or photographer who supplied it. Checkers cannot rely on agency descriptions. Be skeptical. When checking an article about the former UN weapons inspector Scott Ritter, one checker was handed a photo of Ritter sitting under an Iraqi flag, flanked by two men. The caption from Agence France-Presse read: *Scott Ritter addressing the National Assembly in Baghdad.* But the two men on either side of Ritter did not look like politicians, and the checker decided to look into it further. She talked to Ritter and his assistant about their recollections of the General Assembly and discovered that the photograph was actually taken at a press briefing, and the two men beside Ritter were translators, not politicians.

When photography accompanies an article, there's no reason to assume that the author of the piece has seen the photograph or was with the photographer at the time the picture was taken. Because the author usually knows more about the subject of the photograph than the photographer does, it may make sense to check the photo first with the author of the piece. Get permission from your editor before you do this. Describe the photograph over the phone or fax it to the author if you can't show it to him or her in person. Then do more careful checking with other sources.

You should not rely on the author as the sole source for checking the photograph if you can possibly help it. In the case of Michael Finkel's "Is Youssouf Malé a Slave?" article in *The New York Times Magazine*, the tip-off that the article had significant factual problems, including composite characters, came when, after publication, a human rights organization involved with Malé's case called to say that the photograph Finkel had taken and identified as being of Youssouf Malé was *not* of Malé. If the photograph could have been checked before publication, the article's integrity would have been questioned earlier, too. But the checker couldn't contact Malé or other key sources to discuss the photo. As Finkel was both author and photographer, there was little chance the deception could be caught.

Whenever possible, call the subject(s) of a portrait. When

photographer Richard Avedon was preparing to publish a book of his period portraits from the sixties, it was only when researchers called the artist Anita Steckel to check a biographical entry accompanying her portrait that they discovered she had no recollection of ever having had her picture taken by Avedon. Although the biographical information about the photograph was accurate with regard to Steckel, the photo turned out to be of another artist with the same first name. If Avedon's studio hadn't arranged for fact-checking, the face might forever have been attached to the wrong name. The biographical information about Steckel could have been confirmed by press clippings or her gallery, but only speaking to her revealed the fundamental problem: The photo was not of her.

When incorrect identifications get into print, the fault is often with the source of the shot. Photo developers can be wrong. A photo developer switched the identifications of photographs of a substance abuse center and a house belonging to Roseanne Barr, and the two were captioned incorrectly in *Entertainment Weekly*. A call to the substance abuse center or to Barr's office would have cleared up the confusion.

With a group photograph or photographs that run side-by-side, the most frequent error is that identifications are reversed. Sometimes the reversal is obvious. The subjects may be people of different sexes, in which case their names will probably indicate which name should be attached to which person. But what about a portrait of two brothers? In that case, the checker should call at least one of them and confirm identities by asking about what clothing was worn at the shoot or other visible differences.

If the photograph was taken further in the past, you may need to check using other methods. *The New Yorker* published a group photograph of Hitler with friends and misidentified Hitler's mistress Eva Braun. Although Braun is of course no longer alive, there are reliable biographies of Hitler with photographs of Braun that a checker could have used for comparison. If the comparison was not conclusive, a copy of the photograph about to be published could have been shown to a biographer or other expert for his or her opinion.

As knowledgeable as a reporter or fact checker may become about the subject of a piece, sometimes an expert really is necessary to make sure that an illustration or photograph is appropriate and described accurately. *National Geographic* once published an article by Dag Hammarskjold about his helicopter trip to Mount Everest. Unfortunately, an accompanying photograph showed the wrong mountain. To avoid such problems when checking photographs of, say, obscure archaeological sites, the magazine's researchers confirm the photographer's information with people on the ground in the location or with experts who have visited the site. A science writer at *Time* says that there have been instances when a reporter has not been specific enough when describing which photograph was needed to illustrate a story, and the magazine has subsequently published photos of, say, the wrong cancer cells. Again, an expert eye would know that the cells weren't exactly what the caption described, and it would be easy enough to fax a copy of the photograph to an appropriate source.

The Importance of Looking at Art Carefully

Sometimes even experts can miss a problem that is obvious to the most ignorant eye. It can be easy to forget to look at photographs carefully. Scrutinize the picture and see if the description seems accurate to you. A researcher at *National Geographic* did nearly everything right when checking a photograph of some NASA astronauts training in zero gravity. The caption said that the astronauts were playing with a jump rope, so the researcher sent the photo and caption to NASA for confirmation, which was given. After the photograph was published, however, a reader wrote a letter saying, in effect, look again. What the caption described as a jump rope was actually a long strand of toothpaste squeezed from a tube and floating in the air. Neither the researcher nor NASA had looked closely at the photograph, but the error was obvious to everyone who did.

Dates of Photographs

The date of a photograph must be accurate and appropriate to the piece it accompanies. Even if the date is not going to be printed in the caption, the checker should be sure to find out the date and think about its significance to the story. For instance, alongside a fashion piece making fun of celebrities who were still wearing just-out-of-fashion pashmina shawls, Joan Rivers was shown wearing the offending garment. But the joke was on the newspaper that printed the piece. As Rivers's PR person was delighted to point out, the photograph, rather than Rivers's fashion sense, was a year behind the times. Be skeptical of the date provided by a photographer or photo agency. Look carefully at the date and at the photograph. Do the two seem to be in agreement?

Analyzing the Implications of Photographs and Art

The content of a photograph or illustration must match the content of the writing it accompanies. Sometimes photographs help to confirm or correct facts in the body of the text. A photograph of a building, for example, might help clarify how the structure should be described by the author. A checker should always compare the text and the art to be sure that they do not contradict each other in any way. An even more serious concern, however, is whether the art implies something that the author does not go so far as to state in the text. There is a particular danger that this may occur if an early draft of the piece had stated facts or drawn conclusions that were later taken out because of fact-checking concerns.

Some art may be construed as libelous, so check pictures as carefully for accuracy as the text they accompany. As with printed text, libelous pictorial material can be very broadly defined as casting aspersions on character or professionalism, causing the subject to be reviled or ridiculed, or damaging his or her ability to earn money. (Definitions of what is libelous differ from state to state; checkers should discuss any concerns with counsel.) When *Esquire* magazine was preparing to publish an article on drugs in the suburbs, their researchers were concerned about photographs chosen to accompany the story. One showed a car filled with smoke in a suburban street. The checkers worried that the house shown in the background of the photograph was identifiable (since the owners could feel that the photograph cast aspersions upon their own habits), and whether the car license plate and street signs might be legible. Checkers should be alert for this sort of innuendo. Keep art from suggesting that a man who has yet to be tried is guilty (by portraying him behind bars), or depicting a subject involved in any unsavory activity that cannot be supported by fact.

Checking Captions and Headlines

Caption checking is just like any other text checking, but because captions and headlines are so prominent, it is particularly important to get them right. Names and dates are especially sensitive. Captions and headlines often give the reader a distilled form of the article, so do not misstate or exaggerate the article's claims. If the sources backing up a particular fact in the body of the piece are weak but are to be included in the published version despite checking concerns, try to keep those facts out of the captions and headlines, where they will be particularly noticeable.

Captions tend to become a problem because they are usually one of the last additions to a piece before it is published. If you check a caption before you finish checking the piece, look at the caption again just before closing to be sure that you haven't found any late information that renders it incorrect. If the caption is a quotation from the piece, be certain that the quotation as it appears in the body of the piece has not been altered during editing or fact-checking.

Checking Maps

Fact checkers look at maps to be certain that information such as name spellings and distances are consistent with those mentioned in the article. The outline of the country or area on the map and the location of named places or features should be checked against a reliable atlas or map. If the article mentions five national parks in a mapped area, then checkers should be sure that the map shows the locations of those five parks. Previously published maps are protected by copyright, so resemblances between the new map and the published source map cannot be too close.

Checking Video Documentaries

Video documentaries require a high standard of fact-checking, though this is often done by associate producers and producers rather than by people whose sole job is to fact check. The checking routine is nearly identical to that for print journalism. "We operate very much like a news organization," says Paul Gallagher, a producer at VH1's *Behind the Music*. Gallagher says that the show uses high-level fact-checking. When someone says that something occurred in a particular year, the date is checked, and if it is off, the comment is edited out of the program. When a subject says something about someone else, the producers will go to the second party to get his or her response. The producers do use Nexis for research, "but it's amazing how many things get reported incorrectly, over and over again. A good example is a story about the band TLC. They were having a big battle with their manager. All the published reports said the manager had sued them for $10 million. But VH1 actually went to the court and got the suit and found out that it was in fact a $40 million suit—a significant difference." If an assertion is documented, VH1 sees what the original document says. "We pull police reports, wills, arrest records, and lawsuits all the time. The music industry is very litigious and we want to get our facts right. When we were doing a show about Julian Lennon, he said that Yoko Ono was screwing him out of his father's money. We pulled John Lennon's will and it turned out that indeed John Lennon had left the disbursement of the estate largely up to Yoko. Then we got a source close to Yoko to tell us that she dealt with money for the children pretty evenhandedly. And of course we talked to Yoko's lawyer."

Fact-Checking a News Program

Looking closely at reputable news programs, one can see that though there may not be any fact checkers, there is a lot of fact-checking being done, often by very senior staff. Take *The NewsHour with Jim Lehrer*, a television program broadcast each weeknight on public broadcasting stations across the country. Relative to other news programs, the show has a small staff. Because it is broadcast live, the interview portion of the program really can't be fact-checked, although the anchors formulate their questions with the help of the research department, which consists of just three people and a few young desk assistants. The researchers use newspaper clips, books, Web searches, and existing files from the show's library to create packets of information on subjects the anchors want to discuss. Before the information is given to the anchors, it is vetted by Annette Miller, the director of research and information services. Like a fact checker, she assesses the value of the sources the researchers have gathered ("If it's off the Internet I'll often throw it out," she says). Again, like a checker, she'll talk to the anchors about how reliable certain facts are—or aren't—so that the anchors can make informed decisions about what to use. The show also contains a news segment, which summarizes the day's news. In this case, it's the senior producer for news, Russ Clarkson, who does the fact-checking. Once his reporters turn in their summaries, he scrutinizes their sources. "I check the original documents: wires, transcripts, statements," he says. "We're leery of unnamed sources. If the source isn't named, we look for a second source to back up that information." He takes it for granted that reporters are checking while they write, but he checks too, and will look at a reporter's notes if necessary.

Different programs fact check differently. Robert Read, who is senior producer for the investigative unit at *Inside Edition*, describes a process in which the researcher (who is known as the story coordinator) and the producer work as a team on a story from the initial concept to its release on air. They gather all the facts for a story using Nexis and wire services and identify and contact people for interviews. The researcher and the producer are responsible for the accuracy of the finished story. Unlike the live interviews in a daily news program, interviews on *Inside Edition* programs are edited prior to airing. After the reporter conducts interviews with the subjects of the piece, the producer writes a draft of the program, which is then read by the senior producer and the on-air reporter. They will query facts and when necessary double-check transcripts. Once the senior producer approves the first draft, lawyers vet it for legal concerns. Then the script goes to the editing room, where sound and images are added to the story. These additions present a new layer of concerns about factual accuracy. Though they do not stage re-creations, the *Inside Edition* staff does use footage and images to illustrate the story, which could confuse the viewer. Read says, "We might say that a particular child was brutally attacked in a playground. If we added stock camera shots from a playground that had a close-up of a child, it might give the impression that that was the real child involved." The production staff as a whole fact checks the program right up to the airing date.

Esther Kartiganer, a senior editor at CBS, describes setting up a "standard keeping" protocol at *60 Minutes* in the wake of a lawsuit in 1983. Producers and associate producers do their own fact-checking, but Kartiganer's protocol requires that someone unfamiliar with the material must assess the accuracy of the story. "The problem," she says, "was that the reporting was solid but the editing wasn't, and violated CBS news editing guidelines." She reads all the transcripts used for a *60 Minutes* piece before she sees the cut story. She makes sure that the cut story fairly represents the transcripts. For example, she might want to check that the quotation used on tape was originally in answer to the question posed in the narration of the cut story. CBS does not have lawyers review the stories unless the production team asks them to, so a second set of eyes is particularly useful. What Kartiganer does is a variety of fact-checking that looks not so much at the details of the story but the overall impression it gives.

Getting Legal Documents from Courts

Looking at original legal documents is crucial when fact-checking a story that involves a lawsuit. Contact lawyers for both parties in a dispute; they are often a good source for copies of relevant legal documents. Checkers sometimes have to go directly to the courts to get legal documents. When producers at VH1 want to read a copy of an original legal document, such as Lennon's will, they often find it through Bruce Lazarus, the president of LegalEase. Lazarus is an expert at finding legal documents, and his methods are those of a fact checker. If looking for Lennon's will, for example, Lazarus says he would first try to determine where Lennon would have probated his will. Because Lennon lived in New York, Lazarus would start there, at the Surrogate's Court. There he would look up Lennon in the court's card index or computer (later records are indexed on the computer), pull the file, and make a copy. In the case of an arrest, the checker would have to find out where the arrest occurred and then go to the local criminal court to make a copy of the arrest report. "Unless the file is sealed," says Lazarus, "anyone can get a copy." For a lawsuit, he would first figure out where the suit was filed. Lazarus says, "You can do a lot of these searches online, particularly if the case is on the federal level. But of course the online information only goes back so far." He rarely relies solely on the online information. "You really want to see the document itself to make sure what you're getting is one hundred percent accurate." Obtaining birth, death, and marriage certificates requires a "letter of authorization" (probably from a relative or family attorney) that shows you have the right to see the documents. You may also have to pay a fee, and the documents will probably be sent to you through the mail, so you'll need to allow for a few days' delay when scheduling your work.

Fact-Checking Songs and Lyrics

Always double-check information about recorded song author-ship, publisher, and copyright date. This information is avail-able in reference books (see Recommended Sources in Chapter Nine), but the most authoritative source for songs not yet in the public domain (most music published in or before the mid-1920s is now in the public domain) will be one of the three licensing companies that help artists to collect their roy-alties. These are the American Society of Composers, Authors, and Publishers (ASCAP), Broadcast Music Incorporated (BMI), and the Society of European Stage Authors and Composers (SESAC).

Each of these three organizations has an online database that makes it easy to access information about the songs for which they hold licenses. (You may request information by tele-phone, too, but BMI and ASCAP like to restrict calls to ques-tions about three songs, so you may find the databases more practical to use.) Both BMI and ASCAP hold licenses for music by a wide range of artists. When deciding which organi-zation is most likely to hold the license, bear in mind that ASCAP was founded in 1914 and BMI in 1940. ASCAP can be said to dominate licenses for the first half of the twentieth century. Because it was founded, in part, to accommodate artists who did not meet ASCAP's requirements for membership, BMI is generally more responsible for popular music of the forties, such as older country and rhythm and blues songs. Though much smaller than ASCAP and BMI, SESAC, founded in 1930, handles the same variety of work; they no longer specialize in European artists.

ASCAP will provide copyright dates as well as the name of the author and the publisher's name and phone number. BMI and SESAC provide the same information but do not have copyright dates. For copyright dates they will refer you to the music publisher.

Lyrics are copyrighted, so you'll need to get permission before reprinting them. Standards vary as to the length you can quote without permission; discuss this with a lawyer. To be conservative, plan to get permission for any song quotation regardless of length. Permission must be obtained from the music publisher. You can get contact information for the publisher from the relevant licensing organization.

Checking Letters to the Editor

To check letters from readers, check the spelling and accuracy of names and addresses and any facts in the letter. (It is possible for a publication to be sued for libel if a letter it prints is found to be defamatory.) If the reader characterizes, paraphrases, or quotes from the article to which he or she is responding, review the original article and make sure the reader's information about it is correct. If a reader's letter introduces new facts, check them independently. Ask the reader for his or her sources but find other sources as backup. If you feel that the reader's wording needs to be altered, suggest a fix for the problem to the editor. The letter writer should agree to the fix before it can be made.

9

Checking Resources

Assessing the Credibility of Research Materials

Whether you're using an Internet site, a reference book, or a narrative nonfiction book as a source, you'll need to gauge its reliability before trusting its information. While checkers have traditionally preferred books to the Internet, this may be changing. More reference books are becoming available over the Internet, where they can be searched with greater facility. An example of this is books of quotations. The Web site www.bartleby.com allows users to search for quotations within individual volumes, such as *Bartlett's Familiar Quotations*, or within the entire site, which contains many primary sources, including the King James Version of the Bible and a complete Shakespeare. It's far easier to use than a book and just as reliable.

Assessing the Reliability of Reference Books

Some book editors will tell you that books are not as reliable as they once were. Fewer and fewer are fact-checked, one editor says. "Given the increasing demands of product turnaround, the whole business of fact-checking has gone completely by the wayside." There's no way to know to what extent a book has been fact-checked, unless the author or editor refers to a checker in her acknowledgments, and even then, it is quite likely that the checking was selective rather than exhaustive. So, how can you tell whether a book is likely to be a reliable source?

First, consider the reputations of the author and publisher. What does the author description say about the writer or editor? Is the author affiliated with a university? Does she teach the subject about which she's written? Has she written on this subject before? Does the university have a good reputation? Flip through the back of the book to look for a bibliography, the presence of which should be encouraging if the cited books look authoritative. An index is nearly always essential if the book is not arranged alphabetically. Without an index you will waste precious time thumbing through chapter after chapter. Look for footnotes, which can direct you to the author's sources if you need more information on a subject to which the author refers fleetingly. The acknowledgments page will give you a sense of the people the author spoke to in preparing the book. The introduction or preface may contain a discussion of the author's sources and methods.

If the book is a relatively recent one, check on Nexis for reviews of the book to see what kind of critical reception it received. Because book reviews are often written by experts on the book's subject, reviewers may comment on the accuracy of the book. Consider contacting an academic authority on the subject to get his or her opinion of the book's value as a source. Primary sources are, of course, nearly always better than secondary sources, but there is always the danger that a book written by a primary source could lack critical distance and be biased or underreported. If the book has gone into editions, use the latest revision, as it may take into account facts in earlier editions that were challenged by readers or critics.

Assessing the Research Value of Internet Sites

The Internet is full of information, much of which is useful to fact checkers. It's important to use it thoughtfully and attentively so that you do not, in an attempt to get information at top speed, use a source that is not authoritative. Before you take information from a site, ask yourself if you are certain that you know who is responsible for creating the site, what the site is (is it a teenager's book report, or is it a publisher's press release?), where it originated, and when it was created or updated. You might also want to examine the quality of the prose, copyediting, and graphics and the variety of links the site offers to other Web sites.

Speaking very broadly, even good Internet sites seem to

suffer from less thorough copyediting than books do. Do not take a name spelling from an Internet site without double-checking it elsewhere if you can possibly help it. Given sufficient time, use the Internet as a first step in confirming any fact, not just spellings. It's a great medium, but it is simply less trustworthy, overall, than printed or human sources when they are chosen appropriately.

Creating a Checking Rolodex or Source List

Keeping a department-wide Rolodex of useful phone numbers or a list of contact names and numbers in a computer file is a fast and convenient way to make sure that every checker has access to this information. When checkers work with a source they think may be helpful on some other piece, they should contribute the information to the phone list. The list should be annotated with the date of the piece for which the source was initially called, so that another checker calling the source can refer to the previous time when calling. The list should be cross-referenced. If a scholar is an expert on Manet, the listing should go under the name *Manet* but should also be placed under the normal alphabetic listing for the source's last name.

If someone in the department has time, the list can be enriched by a checker leafing through scholarly book reviews for names and affiliations of experts in fields likely to be of use to the department in checking some future piece. After finding out where the expert teaches or works, the checker can call him and ask if he would mind being called with a future fact-checking inquiry. If the expert is receptive to questions, then his name can be added to the list.

How Specific Publications and Resources Are Fact-Checked

It is ironic that many of the best resources for fact checkers are not fact-checked to the standard to which checkers aspire. Yet for various reasons these publications are still first-rate references when combined with other sources. The following is an overview of fact-checking at particular recommended resources.

THE NEW YORK TIMES

The New York Times Magazine is fact-checked by four full-time checkers and additional freelancers, as needed. The magazine checkers verify facts within quotes and in August 2002 began to use the author's notes as sources. The *Times* newspaper is not fact-checked routinely, with the exception of information accompanying restaurant, arts, and entertainment reviews or travel pieces. Assistant Managing Editor Allan Siegal says, "Because of the intense deadline structure of daily journalism, we don't employ fact checkers. . . . Our staff writers are instructed to do their own fact-checking, and to alert the copy desk when they have left a questionable fact unchecked." Copy editors are responsible for checking for consistency within a piece and for checking facts that can be verified in standard reference books. Editors are expected to query facts that seem suspect.

According to Linda Amster, the research news manager at the paper, the *Times* was the first U.S. newspaper to employ a staff of full-time researchers. About a dozen research librarians are available to any member of the staff to check particular facts that require time-consuming verification. What they do is technically research because it precedes the writing of a manuscript; they provide information rather than check facts. The researchers are based in the largest newspaper reference library in the country. It contains about 60,000 volumes, some dating back to the mid-nineteenth century. The research librarians subscribe to perhaps 200 periodicals, from *People* magazine to esoteric scholarly journals, and they have access to research databases beyond those available at the writers' desks.

THE WASHINGTON POST

Staff writers for *The Washington Post* newspaper get research assistance from research and library staff. A number of desks, including the foreign, national, investigative, financial, and metro desks, have a resident specialist researcher. Writers who work for desks that don't have a resident researcher can request help from one of seven or eight researchers in the library. The library is open and staffed seven days a week until the paper goes to press. Research Editor Margot Williams says researchers will research anything, but spend much of their time identifying potential sources through online databases. They also create databases on special subjects, such as campaign finance. They will draft spreadsheets from their research and supply information for charts and timelines. They never call sources themselves, which only a reporter may do. They do not fact check written pieces, but they do fact check *Washington Post* books and special projects for the paper, such as a six-part series on Enron.

The Washington Post magazine relies upon its copy desk to check facts. There are no fact checkers as such. The head of the copy desk, John Cotter, says that each of the three copy editors has about three days to work on a story. They check names and dates and facts within quotes. Authors are responsible for their own facts. If the copy editors cannot confirm something that worries them, they will ask the author, "We have not been able to verify this in print. Do you stand by it?" They can request that the author go back to his notes and double-check his facts. (The copy editors do not get source material from the author unless there's a legal issue.) A research department is available to find facts for authors.

TIME

The newsweekly *Time* once employed researchers whose sole job it was to research and fact check all the stories that ran in the magazine. Over the past twenty years, the role of these researchers has broadened to include some writing, and the researchers have become known as reporters. The thirty-odd

reporters who now work at *Time* support the work of the nominal writers, whose ranks most reporters hope someday to join.
Reporters do preliminary story research and reporting with
the help of correspondents who report on the ground from
places other than New York, where *Time* is based, and with
the assistance of eight research librarians who are particularly
adept at data retrieval. Reporters assemble a file of relevant
information that the writer then uses to compile his or her
story. Reporters have little direct contact with primary sources;
such interviews are conducted by the writer. During the writing process the writer or the editor may ask the reporter to
find additional information for the story. After the story is
completed, the same reporter will fact check the story, largely
relying on the file he or she had originally compiled. The
photo department is responsible for confirming information in
captions, although reporters must confirm proper names. In-
house lawyers read everything that will be published in the
magazine, and if they find anything of concern, they quiz
reporters about their sources.

In the past, every piece of copy published in *Time* was
researched and fact-checked. Now about 50 percent of the
pieces are fact-checked by the writers themselves, and some
writers do not even use reporters to help with their preliminary research. Whether a piece is checked by a reporter seems
to depend upon the length of the story—longer pieces generally
requiring more checking—and the amount of time the writer
had to research and write the story.

THE ECONOMIST

The Economist magazine, which appears weekly, has thirteen researchers working in its London office, with more overseas in Washington, D.C., New York, Frankfurt, Tokyo, Singapore, and other satellite offices. Their fact-checking used to be very light, but the head of the desk says it "grew like Topsy." Writers are responsible for their own facts, but the research department checks statistics, charts, names, and dates. They do not ask for journalists' notes, and they don't call sources to confirm quotations. Researchers become quite expert in their respective sections. Most of them are trained as economists or statisticians.

SCIENTIFIC AMERICAN

Scientific American is a monthly magazine for educated laymen that bridges the challenging divide between journalism and the content of peer-reviewed science journals. About 60 percent of the copy is written by experts, with the remaining pieces written by journalists who are knowledgeable about their subjects to varying degrees. The magazine employs one full-time researcher who fact checks names, affiliations, and all numbers and does more thorough investigation of anything controversial. The work of this researcher is augmented by other staff and freelancers who do fact-checking for at least some of their working hours. If an expert scientist is writing about his field, the researchers will not check everything she or he writes, because they assume a high level of knowledge. When a journalist is the author, however, the researchers will gauge the level of expertise and have experts vet paragraphs or the entire piece. Researchers also check original material that appears on the *Scientific American* Web site.

WORLD ALMANAC

The *World Almanac* does not have staff dedicated exclusively to fact-checking. They have several editors and use freelance help in collecting material, which they later check. They tend to use primary sources. Checking is done against the original source to make sure it has been accurately transcribed. The *Almanac* isn't 100 percent checked, says editor Bill McGeveran. "We wouldn't necessarily go the last mile if it didn't seem suspicious." Editors insert source lines so that readers can tell where material came from.

Recommended Sources

Checkers use all kinds of sources for their work. In addition to the materials authors provide them with, checkers may ask experts in particular subjects for their suggestions for trustworthy source material. Checking that requires very detailed, extensive information on a single subject will obviously require books that focus on that subject. However, checkers often use general reference books for cross-checking information. The following is a highly subjective list of reference books and resources that have proved useful and reliable. Remember that it is always a good idea to check the same information in more than one source to be sure that the information agrees. If it does not, pursue the facts elsewhere. No source, primary or secondary, is infallible.

Note: Some of the Internet sources listed provide full information only to subscribers.

ADVERTISING

The John W. Hartman Center for Sales, Advertising, and Marketing
History at Duke University
http://scriptorium.lib.duke.edu/hartman
Telephone: 919 660-5827

McDonough, John, and Karen Egolf, eds., *The Advertising Age Encyclopedia of Advertising*. Chicago: Fitzroy Dearborn Publishers, 2002.

Museum of Advertising & Design
208 North Water St.
Milwaukee, WI 53202
Telephone: 414 847-3290
Fax: 414 847-3299

ART AND ARCHITECTURE

Calloway, Stephen, and Elizabeth Cromley, eds. *The Elements of Style: A Practical Encyclopedia of Interior Architectural Details from 1485 to the Present*. New York: Simon & Schuster, 1997.

Fleming, John, Nicolaus Pevsner, and Hugh Honour. *The Penguin Dictionary of Architecture and Landscape*. London and New York: Penguin, 1999.

Langmuir, Erika, and Norbert Lynton. *The Yale Dictionary of Art and Artists*. New Haven: Yale University Press, 2000.

BALLET

The International Dictionary of Ballet, Farmington Hills, MI: St. James Press, 2002.

BUSINESS

Gale Directory of Publications and Broadcast Media. Detroit, MI: Gale, 2002.

Hoover's: www.hoovers.com
   Invaluable source for company profiles, contact information, and press releases, with links to competitors.

Hoover's MasterList of Major U.S. Companies. Austin, TX: Hoover's Business Press, 2001. Any book in this series will be useful.

FOOD

Kiple, Kenneth, and Kriemhild Coneè Ornelas. *The Cambridge World History of Food*. Cambridge, UK; New York: Cambridge University Press, 2000.

Montagné, Prosper, ed. *Larousse Gastronomique*. New York: Clarkson N. Potter, 2001.

GENERAL REFERENCE

Atterberry, Tara E. *Encyclopedia of Associations: International Associations*. Farmington Hills, MI: Gale, 2002.

Facts on File: World News Digest with Cumulative Index. New York: Facts on File News Services, a division of the World Almanac Education Group. Weekly.

Hunt, Kimberly N. *Encyclopedia of Associations.* Farmington Hills, MI: Gale, 2002.

Legasse, Paul, et al. *The Columbia Encyclopedia.* New York: Columbia University Press, 2000.

Park, Ken. *World Almanac and Book of Facts.* New York: World Almanac Publications. Annual.

HISTORY

Foner, Eric, and John A. Garrety, eds. *The Reader's Companion to American History.* Boston: Houghton Mifflin, 1991.

Niewyk, Donald L., and Francis R. Nicosia. *The Columbia Guide to the Holocaust.* New York: Columbia University Press, 2000.

Weinberg, Gerhard L. *A World At Arms: A Global History of World War II.* Cambridge, UK; New York: Cambridge University Press, 1995.

Zinn, Howard. *A People's History of the United States: 1492 to Present.* New York: Perennial, 2001.

LIBRARIES

Bodleian Library: www.bodley.ox.ac.uk
Library of Congress: www.loc.gov
New York Public Library: www.nypl.org

LITERATURE

Benét, William Rose, and Bruce Murphy, eds. *Benét's Reader's Encyclopedia.* New York: HarperCollins, 1996.

Brewer, Ebenezer, et al. *Brewer's Dictionary of Phrase and Fable.* New York: HarperCollins, 2000.

Collins, Huam. *Thesaurus of Book Digests: Digests of the World's Permanent Writings from the Ancient Classics to Current Literature.* New York: Outlet, 1998.

Drabble, Margaret. *Oxford Companion to English Literature.* Oxford, UK; New York: Oxford University Press, 2000. (See also companions to literature of other languages.)

Nobel Prize in Literature: www.nobel.se/literature/

Room, Adrian (compiler). *Brewer's Dictionary of Modern Phrase and Fable.* London: Cassell Academic, 2001.

MEDICINE

Beers, Mark H., and Robert Berkow, et al., eds. *The Merck Manual of Diagnosis and Therapy.* Whitehouse Station, NJ: Merck & Co., 1999. Online: www.merck.com/pubs/mmanual/

Blakemore, Colin, and Sheila Jennett, eds. *The Oxford Companion to the Body.* Oxford, UK; New York: Oxford University Press, 2002.

Lyons, Albert J., et al. *Medicine: An Illustrated History.* New York: Abrams, 1987.

National Institutes of Health books and Web site: www.nih.gov

National Library of Medicine, MedLine: www.nlm.nih.gov
    Contains a searchable database of historical materials, drug information, and many other useful facts.

PDR: Physician's Desk Reference. Montvale, NJ: Medical Economics Company. Annual. A comprehensive prescription drug reference book, which includes thorough pharmacological information as well as photographs of pills and other drugs.

MILITARY INFORMATION

Armada International: www.armada.ch
    A weaponry magazine with selected text available online.

The Center for Defense Information: www.cdi.org

The Center for Nonproliferation Studies at the Monterey Institute of
    International Studies: www.cns.miis.edu
Jane's Information Online: www.janes.com
    Defense and weaponry articles and information from a pub-
    lisher of expensive but authoritative specialist books.
Naval Historical Center: www.history.navy.mil
The Oxford Essential Dictionary of the U.S. Military. New York:
    Berkley, 2001.
U.S. Air Force Historical Research Agency: www.maxwell.af.mil/au/
    afhra
U.S. Army Center of Military History: www.army.mil/cmh-pg

MOVIES AND MOVIE ACTORS

Craddock, Jim, ed. *VideoHound's Golden Movie Retriever.* Farming-
    ton Hills, MI: Gale, 2002.
Internet Movie Database: www.imdb.com
    Includes complete listings of films by particular actors. It also
    provides information such as short biographies, lists of role
    names, and guest appearances.
Katz, Ephraim, et al. *The Film Encyclopedia: The Most Comprehen-
    sive Encyclopedia of World Cinema in a Single Volume.* New
    York: HarperResource, 2001.
The Numbers: www.the-numbers.com
    Includes box office receipt listings and other film business
    records.
Screen Actors Guild (SAG): www.sag.org
    For agent information.
Thompson, David. *The New Biographical Dictionary of Film.* New
    York: Knopf, 2002. A more subjective, less exhaustive guide
    than *Halliwell's,* but very reliable.
Variety magazine: www.variety.com
    Contains film reviews dating back to 1914. Although use is on
    a subscription basis, it is free to print subscribers and some
    information is available free to all users.

Walker, John, ed. *Halliwell's Film and Video Guide*. New York: HarperResource, 2001.

——. *Halliwell's Who's Who in the Movies*. New York: Harper-Resource, 2001.

Wiley, Mason, et al. *Inside Oscar: The Unofficial History of the Academy Awards*. New York: Ballantine, 1996. (See also *Inside Oscar 2*, a sequel, published in 2002.)

MUSIC

Clarke, Donald. *The Penguin Encyclopedia of Popular Music*. London; New York: Penguin, 1999.

Hischak, Thomas S. *The Tin Pan Alley Song Encyclopedia:* Westport, CT: Greenwood Publishing Group, 2002.

Kernfeld, Barry, ed. *The New Grove Dictionary of Jazz*. New York: Grove's Dictionaries, 2002.

Kennedy, Michael. *The Oxford Dictionary of Music*. Oxford, UK; New York: Oxford University Press, 1995.

Musical America International Dictionary of the Performing Arts. Contains information on performers, musical venues, agents, etc. Online: www.musicalamerica.com

Sadie, Stanley, ed. *The New Grove Dictionary of Music and Musicians*. New York: Grove's Dictionaries, 2000.

——. *The New Grove Dictionary of Opera*. New York: Grove's Dictionaries, 1998.

Rock 'n' Roll

Robbins, Ira A., ed. *The Trouser Press Guide to '90s Rock*. New York: Fireside/Simon & Schuster, 1997.

Romanowski, Patricia, and Holly George-Warren. *The New Rolling Stone Encyclopedia of Rock & Roll*. New York: Fireside/Rollingstone Press, 2001.

Whitburn, Joel, ed. *The Billboard Book of Top 40 Hits*. New York: Billboard/Watson-Guptill Publications, 2000. (See this series for books on other music styles.)

Songs and Lyrics

The Great Rock Fake Book: Over 250 Songs. Miami, FL: Warner
   Brothers, 1995.

The Harry Fox Agency, Inc.: www.songfile.com
   Includes information on songwriters, license holders, recording artists, album titles, and album playlists.

Herder, Ronald. *500 Best-Loved Song Lyrics.* Mineola, NY: Dover,
   1998.

Kilgarriff, Michael. *Sing Us One of the Old Songs: A Guide to Popular Songs, 1860–1920.* Oxford, UK; New York: Oxford University Press, 1999.

Lax, Roger, and Frederick Smith. *The Great Song Thesaurus.*
   Oxford, UK; New York: Oxford University Press, 1989.

Music Licensing Companies

ASCAP: The American Society of Composers, Authors, and Publishers
www.ascap.com
Telephone: 212 621-6000

BMI: Broadcast Music Incorporated
www.bmi.com
Telephone: 212 586-2000

SESAC: The Society of European Stage Authors and Composers
www.sesac.com
Telephone: 800 826-9996

PEOPLE

Kidd, Charles, and David Williamson. *Debrett's Peerage and Baronetage.* New York: St. Martin's Press and London: Debrett's Peerage Ltd., 2003.

Mosley, Charles, ed. *Burke's Peerage, Baronetage, and Knightage.*
   Crans, Switzerland: Burke's Peerage Ltd., 2003.

The Social Register. New York: Social Register Association, 2002.

Thompson, Clifford. *Current Biography Yearbook.* New York and Dublin: H.W. Wilson Co. Annual.

Who's Who in America. A good preliminary source for personal and career information. New Providence, New Jersey: Marquis Who's Who. Annual.

PHOTOGRAPHY

AP Photo Archive: photoarchive.ap.org
If your media organization has a password, you can view many photographs on this useful site.

QUOTATIONS

Bartlett, John and Justin Kaplan, eds., *Bartlett's Familiar Quotations.* Boston: Little, Brown & Co., 1992.

www.bartleby.com
Invaluable searchable database, which includes the great books of quotations, a complete Shakespeare, the King James Version of the Bible, and many other useful links and texts. A tremendous timesaver.

Knowles, Elizabeth. *The Oxford Dictionary of Quotations.* Oxford, UK; New York: Oxford University Press, 1999.

RADIO

Dunning, John. *On the Air: The Encyclopedia of Old-Time Radio.* Oxford, UK; New York: Oxford University Press, 1998.

SPORTS

www.baseball-reference.com
> Historical baseball statistics compiled by a professor of mathematics and computing.

CBS SportsLine: www.sportsline.com
> Searchable sports news from CBS.

Carroll, Bob, et al., eds. *Total Football II: The Official Encyclopedia of the National Football League.* New York: HarperCollins, 1999.

Diamond, Dan, et al., eds. *Total Hockey: The Official Encyclopedia of the National Hockey League.* Kingston, NY: Total Sports, 2002.

ESPN: www.espn.com

Jordan, Michael. *The Official NBA Encyclopedia.* New York: Doubleday, 2000.

National Basketball Association: www.nba.com

National Football League: www.nfl.com

National Hockey League: www.nhl.com

The Olympic Games: Athens 1896–Sydney 2000. New York: DK Publishing, 2000.

Thorn, John, et al., eds. *Total Baseball: The Official Encyclopedia of Major League Baseball.* Kingston, NY: Total Sports, 2001.

TELEVISION

Brown, Les. *Les Brown's Encyclopedia of Television,* 3rd edition. Farmington Hills, MI: Gale Research Inc., 1992.

Brooks, Tim, and Earle Marsh. *The Complete Directory to Prime Time Network and Cable TV Shows.* New York: Ballantine Books, 1999.

The Emmys: www.emmys.com
> Web site of the Academy of Television Arts and Sciences.

Lenburg, Jeff, et al. *The Encyclopedia of Animated Cartoons.* New York: Facts on File, 1999.

McNeil, Alex. *Total Television: The Comprehensive Guide to Programming from 1948 to the present.* New York: Penguin USA, 1996.

Newcomb, Horace, ed. *Museum of Broadcast Communications Encyclopedia of Television.* Chicago and London: Fitzroy Dearborn, 1997.

O'Neil, Thomas. *The Emmys: The Ultimate, Unofficial Guide to the Battle of TV's Best Shows and Greatest Stars.* New York: Perigee, 2000.

THEATER

Hawkins-Dady, Mark, and David Pickering, eds. *International Dictionary of Theater, Vols 1–3,* Chicago and London: St. James Press, 1992.

Internet Broadway Database: www.ibdb.com

Has production information for Broadway shows dating back to the nineteenth century. Usefully cross-referenced, it also contains basic biographical information.

Norton, Richard C. *A Chronology of American Musical Theatre.* Oxford, UK; New York: Oxford University Press, 2002.

Playbill: www.playbill.com

Contains listings for Broadway and off-Broadway shows. Also links to specific theater Web sites, Tony awards site, etc.

Tony Awards: www.tonyawards.com

Has a searchable database of past winners as well as video clips and photographs.

U.S. GOVERNMENT

Almanac of American Politics. Washington: National Journal. Annual.

Essential source for information on senators, representatives, and governors. Thorough profiles include information on how each official voted in key votes. Also included are election results and descriptions, both statistical and narrative, of the geographical areas they represent. Contains an index.

Brinkley, Alan, and Davis Dyer. *The Reader's Companion to the American Presidency.* Boston: Houghton Mifflin, 2000.

Congress: www.congress.org

Census Bureau: www.census.gov

Congressional Quarterly: Washington Information Directory and other books published by CQ Press such as *CQ Politics in America, CQ Guide to Congress, CQ Guide to the Supreme Court* and *CQ Guide to the Presidency.*

Consumer Price Index Converter: stats.bls.gov

Cornog, Evan, and Richard Whelan. *Hats in the Ring: An Illustrated History of American Presidential Campaigns.* New York: Random House, 2000.

Department of Justice: www.usdoj.gov

   Statistics, information on current investigations, etc.

Federal Election Commission: www.fec.gov

Fed World: www.fedworld.gov

   A gateway to a wealth of official information, from the complete texts of Supreme Court decisions dating back to the 1930s, to federal agency sites and federal economic, social, and educational statistics.

House of Representatives: www.house.gov

Legislative Information: http://thomas.loc.gov

Senate: www.senate.gov

Statistics: www.fedstats.gov

Statistical Abstract of the United States. U.S. Department of Commerce Economics and Statistics Administration. Annual.

U.S. Securities and Exchange Commission: www.sec.gov

The Yellow Book Series. Fourteen books in all, including Congressional, Federal, State, Municipal, and Judicial. New York and Washington: Leadership Directories, Inc. Annuals. Reliable names, titles, and contact information for officials and their staffs. Using the direct dial phone numbers contained in the books makes for more efficient checking.

White House: www.whitehouse.gov

   Biographical information on current administration members, statements, press briefings, and much more.

WINE

Robinson, Jancis, et al., eds. *The Oxford Companion to Wine.* Oxford, UK; New York: Oxford University Press, 1999.

Johnson, Hugh. *Hugh Johnson's Pocket Wine Book 2003.* New York: Mitchell Beazley, 2002.

THE WORLD

Banks, Arthur S., and Thomas C. Muller, eds. *Political Handbook of the World.* Binghampton, NY: Binghampton University. Annual.

CIA World Factbook: www.cia.gov/cia/publications/factbook

Cohen, Saul B. *The Columbia Gazetteer of the World.* New York: Columbia University Press, 2000.

The Europa World Year Book. London: Europa Publications. Annual. Like the *Political Handbook of the World, The Europa World Year Book*s include population information, recent history, names of ministries, and much other useful information organized by country. Each series has its strengths. The Europa books seem to contain more detailed information in certain areas, such as population statistics by principal towns, rather than just nationally, and telephone, fax, and e-mail information.

National Geographic Atlas of the World. Washington, DC: National Geographic Society, 1999.

Natural Resources Defense Council: www.nrdc.org

Turner, Barry, ed. *The Statesman's Year-Book.* London: Palgrave Macmillan. Annual.

The United Nations Statistics Division: http://unstats.un.org/unsd/

Bibliography

Alderman, Ellen, and Caroline Kennedy. "Can a Journalist's Novel Be Libelous?" *Columbia Journalism Review*, July/August 1997.

Ambrose, Stephen. "Tom Hanks: Man with a Mission." *Reader's Digest*, September 2001.

American Journalism Review, December 1995.

Amster, Linda, and Dylan Loeb McClain, eds. *Kill Duck Before Serving: Red Faces at* The New York Times. New York: St. Martin's Press, 2002.

Barnes, Julian. *Letters from London*. New York: Vintage, 1995.

Baron, Sandra S. "Law, the Media & . . . Libel: Old Concerns Renewed." *Columbia Journalism Review*, September/October 2000.

Beam, Alex. "Tabloid Law." *The Atlantic Monthly*, August 1999.

Besenjak, Cheryl. *Copyright Plain and Simple*. Franklin Lakes, NJ: Career Press, 1997.

Bowers, Neal. *Words for the Taking: The Hunt for a Plagiarist*. New York: Norton, 1997.

Bredemeier, Kenneth. "Panel Reinstates Libel Decision Against Post." *The Washington Post*, April 10, 1985.

Brill, Steve. "Rewind." *Brill's Content*, July/August 1999.

Brock, David. "The Slur Against Hillary Clinton." *The New York Times*, July 20, 2000.

Kimberly Bryson v. News America Publications, Inc., 174 Ill 2d.

Busch, Frederick. "Truth, Lies, Fact, Fiction." *The American Scholar*, Summer 2000.

Busch, Noel F. *Briton Hadden: A Biography of the Co-Founder of Time*. New York: Farrar, Straus and Company, 1949.

Carvajal, Doreen. "The Great Quote Question: How much tampering with quotations can journalists ethically do?" *Fineline: The Newsletter on Journalism Ethics*, Vol. 3, No. 1, January 1991.

Crawford, Tad, and Tony Lyons. *The Writer's Legal Guide*. New York: Allworth Press, 1997.

Doonan, Simon. "Denise and Daughter: Isn't It Rich?" *The New York Observer*, March 12, 2001.

Epstein, Joseph. *Narcissus Leaves the Pool: Familiar Essays*. New York: Houghton Mifflin, 1999.

Finkel, Michael. "Is Youssouf Malé a Slave?" *The New York Times Magazine*, November 18, 2001.

Foer, Franklin. "Gail Sheehy, Journalism's Id." *The New Republic*, October 9, 2000.

Garner, Dwight. "Beg, Borrow, Or . . . " Salon.com, http://www.salon.com/weekly/plagiarism960722.html

Gibaldi, Joseph. *MLA Handbook for Writers of Research Papers*, Fifth Edition. New York: The Modern Language Association of America, 1999.

Goldstein, Norm, ed. *The Associated Press Stylebook and Briefing on Media Law*, Cambridge, MA: Perseus, 2000.

Gross, Jane. "Editor Recalls Overriding Lawyer on a Quotation in Dispute." *The New York Times*, May 20, 1993.

Hanson, Christopher. "The New New Journalism." *Columbia Journalism Review*, November/December 1999.

Hartsock, John C. *A History of American Literary Journalism*. Amherst: University of Massachusetts, 2000.

Heidenry, John. *Theirs Was the Kingdom: Lila and DeWitt Wallace and the Story of the* Reader's Digest. New York: W. W. Norton and Company, 1993.

Herbert v. Lando. 568 f.2d 974 (2d Circuit 1977), 441 U.S. 153 (1979), 596 F. Supp. 1178 (SDNY 1984), 781 F.2d 298 (2d Circuit 1986).

Jassin, Lloyd J., and Steven C. Schechter. *The Copyright Permission and Libel Handbook*. New York: John Wiley and Sons, Inc., 1998.

Jeffrey M. Masson, Petitioner v. New Yorker Magazine, Inc., Alfred A. Knopf, Inc., and Janet Malcolm. No. 89-1799 Supreme Court of the United States. 501 U.S. 496; 111 S. Ct. 2419.

Kane, Peter E. *Errors, Lies, and Libel*. Carbondale and Edwardsville: Southern Illinois University Press, 1992.

Kelley, Tina. "Whales in the Minnesota River?" *The New York Times*, March 4, 1999.

Kelly, Keith J. "Scene and Heard." *Daily News*, April 4, 1997.

Kelly, Michael. "The Man of the Minute." *The New Yorker*, July 17, 1995.

Kerrane, Kevin, and Ben Yagoda, eds. *The Art of Fact: A Historical Anthology of Literary Journalism*. New York: Scribner, 1997.

Kirkpatrick, David. "As Historian's Fame Grows, So Does Attention to Sources." *The New York Times*, January 11, 2002.

Kirtley, Jane E. *The First Amendment Handbook*. Arlington, VA: The Reporters Committee for Freedom of the Press, 1999. http://www.rcfp.org/handbook

Kurtz, Howard. "Hoax Exposes Journalism's 'Fast Track'; D.C. now a magnet to ambition, not the truth." *The Washington Post*, May 18, 1998.

Lange v. Australian Broadcasting Corporation (1997) 189 C.L.R. 520.

Lewis, Anthony. *Make No Law: The Sullivan Case and the First Amendment*. New York: Random House, 1991.

Lieberman, Trudy. "Plagiarize, plagiarize, plagiarize, only be sure to always call it research." *Columbia Journalism Review*, July 1995.

Lightcap, Carolina. "Is That a Fact?" *Student Press Review*, Spring 1991.

Lindey, Alexander. *Plagiarism and Originality*. New York: Harper and Brothers, 1952.

Murphy, Cullen. "Fine Points." *The Atlantic Monthly*, March 2001.

Pogrebin, Abigail, and Rifka Rosenwein. "Not the First Time." *Brill's Content*, September 1998.

Pogrebin, Robin. "Rechecking a Writer's Facts, A Magazine Uncovers Fiction." *The New York Times*, June 12, 1998.

Rosman, Katherine. "The Secret of Her Success." *Brill's Content*, November 1998.

Rothman, Rodney. "My Fake Job." *The New Yorker*, November 27, 2000.

Shapiro, Susan. "Caution! This Paper Has Not Been Fact Checked!" Gannett Center for Media Studies, New York.

Shepard, Alicia C. "How Much Is Too Much?" *American Journalism Review*, December 1995.

Smith, Patricia. *The Boston Globe*, June 16, 1998.

Talese, Gay. *Fame and Obscurity*. New York: Ivy Books, 1993.

Urban, Christine D. *Examining Our Credibility: Perspectives of the Public and the Press*. Virginia: A Report for the ASNE Journalism Credibility Project, 1999.

Westin, Av. *Best Practices for Television Journalists*, Freedom Forum's Free Press/Fair Press Project, Arlington, VA. [No copyright date.]

Wicklein, John. "Fun and Profit with Libel: Australia." *Columbia Journalism Review*, November/December 1991.

Windolf, Jim. "Off the Record." *The New York Observer*, October 19, 1992.

Wolfe, Tom, and E. W. Johnson, eds. *The New Journalism*. New York: Harper, 1973.

Yagoda, Ben. *About Town:* The New Yorker *and the World It Made*. New York: Scribner, 2000.

[No author listed.] "News Bigwigs Bamboozled." *Media and the Law*, Vol. 6, No. 10, May 22, 1998.